SpringerBriefs in B

For further volumes:
http://www.springer.com/series/8860

Erik Hofmann · Oliver Belin

Supply Chain Finance Solutions

Relevance—Propositions—Market Value

 Springer

Dr. Erik Hofmann
Chair of Logistics Management
 (LOG-HSG)
University of St.Gallen
Dufourstrasse 40a
9000 St. Gallen
Switzerland
e-mail: erik.hofmann@unisg.ch

Oliver Belin
Sumitomo Mitsui Banking Corporation
 Europe Ltd
99 Queen Victoria Street
London EC4V 4EH
UK
e-mail: oliver_belin@gb.smbcgroup.com

ISSN 2191-5482

e-ISSN 2191-5490

ISBN 978-3-642-17565-7

e-ISBN 978-3-642-17566-4

DOI 10.1007/978-3-642-17566-4

Springer Heidelberg Dordrecht London New York

Cover design: eStudio Calamar, Berlin/Figueres

Printed on acid-free paper

Springer is part of Springer Science+Business Media (www.springer.com)

Management Summary

With widespread coverage in the media, at conferences and in numerous articles in finance magazines, Supply Chain Finance (SCF) has become one of the hottest topics in business administration. SCF is not a recent concept. It has long been known as a significant part at the intersection of Supply Chain Management (SCM) and trade finance. What has changed during recent years is the decision of numerous companies to convert the approach and its opportunities into deliverable benefits.

The rules of the game in trade finance have changed. With the latest credit crisis, companies see their supply chains threatened by a lack of liquidity. This cash dry-up makes corporates look to more tangible sources of financing their businesses. Financial institutions are increasingly responding to corporate demands to increase efficiency in their financial supply chains. With competition no longer among individual companies but among entire supply chains, every area of end-to-end cost reduction is being explored. Therefore, SCF solutions could help leading companies make their whole supply chain more competitive.

Recent research seems to confirm that the credit crunch is driving the adoption of SCF. Both banks and corporates are keener than ever to make their scarce capital stretch as far as possible. The global economic crisis has resulted in reactions that are fueling the widespread adoption of SCF. The credit crunch is making buyers and suppliers deplete their cash positions. Whereas suppliers are trying to encourage their customers to pay earlier, buyers are increasing their payment terms. In an attempt to cope with these problems and fully utilize the value creation potential of a company's supply chain, SCF promises rewards. By taking a more holistic view of flows of trade, this approach focuses on collaboration between trading partners as well as the increased transparency, automation and dematerialization of the entire supply chain, thereby reducing overall costs and risks for all affiliated parties. SCF promises to enhance enterprise value because it decreases tied-up working capital and enables higher capital efficiency.

Because of the novelty of SCF, there are still many research gaps. On the one hand, the lack of research leads to hesitation about the implementation of SCF solutions within companies because there is little quantified evidence about achievable cost savings and other potential benefits. On the other hand, there is very little information about the market potential for SCF solutions.

This study aims at providing orientation within this new topic by investigating the need and nature as well as characteristics and enablers of SCF. Based on an exemplary SCF model, the worldwide market size for such solutions and potential cost savings to companies engaging in this area are analyzed and calculated. These underline the generally stated attractiveness of SCF solutions by creating win–win situations; for the affiliated actors in the end-to-end supply chain as well as for external service providers.

Preface

This book is written for both academicians and practitioners who are interested in Supply Chain Finance. It can also be used as a textbook for seniors and MBA students or for those preparing for examinations at the intersection of supply chain management and trade finance.

Supply Chain Finance has become more and more important during the last years. The effect of globalization of supply chains makes it more challenging than ever for companies to keep their competitive edge. More recently the economic crisis in 2008/2009 resulted in reactions that are fueling the widespread adoption of trade finance due to the scares liquidity and unsound working capital situation of trade partners in the global market place.

This publication provides background on the growing importance of Supply Chain Finance, delving into the key elements and available options from which these solutions are crafted and implemented. While the market for Supply Chain Finance is still in the early stages of development, innovative companies already have made use of it and others will soon follow.

Because of the novelty of this subject, most publications so far have only covered certain parts of Supply Chain Finance and have left many research gaps. This might also explain why some companies still hesitate to use Supply Chain Finance solutions and to reap its benefits.

Our contribution explores the different aspects of Supply Chain Finance and solutions available in the market. It attempts to develop an understanding of how developments in international trade and other drivers have impacted supply chain management and have increased the interest of major corporations to adopt new practices in trade finance and working capital management. In our publication the reader will learn about the different challenges and benefits and the potential market size of Supply Chain Finance solutions as well as get some indications where these practice can be applied in attempts to improve working capital and company value.

It is hoped that readers will appreciate the new insight in Supply Chain Finance in general and the calculated global market potential and market size of the solution in particular.

The valuable comments and support of our colleagues, especially at the Chair of Logistics Management, University of St. Gallen (Switzerland), has been most welcome. At the end, we wishes to acknowledge the generous support of Nathalie and Andrea for the publication of the book.

St. Gallen and London, February 2011   Erik Hofmann
                                                                                             Oliver Belin

Contents

List of Abbreviations

A/P	Accounts payable
A/R	Accounts receivable
C2C	Cash-to-cash
CRM	Credit risk management
ERP	Enterprise resource planning
LIBOR	London interbank offered rate
DPO	Days payables outstanding
DSO	Days sales outstanding
L/C	Letter of credit
OECD	Organization for economic co-operation and development
O/A	Open account
PO	Purchase order
SCF	Supply chain finance
SCM	Supply chain management
SITC	Standard international trade classification
SWIFT	Society for worldwide interbank financial telecommunication
WACC	Weighted average cost of capital
WIP	Work in progress
WCM	Working capital management
SOX	Sarbanes–Oxley

Chapter 1
Introduction

Abstract The study's objectives are to fill part of a research gap in Supply Chain Finance by highlighting potential costs savings and revenue generations for parts of the supply chain as well as to quantify the potential market size for such Supply Chain Finance solutions.

Keywords Supply chain finance · Cost optimization · Competitive advantage · Liquidity · Working capital · Automated trade finance solutions · Internal & external collaboration · Implementation

1.1 Problem Definition and Objectives of the Study

Revolutions, by their very definition, bring about fundamental changes. Arguably such an event is occurring in trade finance with new technology being the tool for transformation. As with all revolutions, such as Supply Chain Finance (SCF), new players emerge proposing different approaches and embracing new business models (Pugsley 2007). SCF is no different. The race is now on to create a viable business model for making money out of SCF solutions. New innovative solutions are poised to make major improvements, making financial flows faster, more reliable, more predictable and more cost efficient (Croft 2007).

Over recent decades, competition in nearly all industries has become more global. To cope with these challenges and also benefit from the resulting opportunities, companies have been forced to become innovation leaders and streamline their organizations by engaging in cost cutting and efficiency improvements. This highly competitive nature and the ongoing battle for cost optimization have placed pressure on every part of a business to generate competitive advantages. With the fall of international trade barriers and the shift from letters of credit to open account (O/A) trading, the introduction of automated trade finance solutions has

E. Hofmann and O. Belin, *Supply Chain Finance Solutions*, SpringerBriefs in Business, DOI: 10.1007/978-3-642-17566-4_1, © Springer-Verlag Berlin Heidelberg 2011

become an important point on corporate agendas (Bougheas et al. 2009). With the current volatile climate and the lack of available credit, innovations in working capital solutions are more vital now than ever before.

Because global competition continues to get tougher and shareholders constantly demand company leaders outperform their peers, further value generation opportunities within a company's supply chain are required. Accompanied by tighter liquidity situations, senior management is increasingly urged to ensure a stronger focus on the financial side of their supply chain and optimize their working capital. When putting these postulations into practice, however, two challenges exist. On the one hand, traditionally available trade finance solutions are either costly themselves or likely to remain with single company benefits while increasing total costs and risks in the end-to-end supply chain. On the other hand, existing, manual processes and paper-based trade finance procedures within corporate organizations make the introduction of new trade finance solutions difficult.

In an attempt to cope with these challenges, the approach of SCF has become gradually more prevalent. It represents solutions available for financing goods and products as they move from origin to final destination along the supply chain. By taking an end-to-end perspective on the whole supply chain, it aims at decreasing its overall costs while fostering internal and external collaboration as well as transparency and automation. Therefore, an engaging company is likely to experience lower costs and a financially more stable end-to-end supply chain, resulting in a strategic advantage (Fairchild 2005).

Because of the novelty of this approach, the piecemeal theoretical coverage of this area started only a couple of years ago. Some initial studies have tried to structure this new approach, but mostly they have only covered certain parts of SCF and have left many research gaps. This lack of thorough theoretical coverage might also explain why some managers still hesitate to implement SCF and to reap its benefits.

The objectives of this study are to fill part of the research gap and to offer an insight on the relevance of SCF by highlighting potential cost savings and revenue opportunities to engaging parties. From the perspective of a supply chain participant, it is crucial to obtain knowledge of the net benefit of SCF and of the required environment that favors the implementation of such solutions.

Since there have not yet been any qualified attempts to quantify the global market potential and market size, this study focuses among others on the following two research questions.

1. How large is the potential market size for SCF solutions?
2. How big are the potential cost savings to companies engaging in SCF solutions?

1.2 Course of Investigation

To gain an overview of the key benefits of SCF the focus of this study is first set on working capital management (WCM) and its contribution towards enhancing enterprise value (Richards and Laughlin 1980). Based on the subsequent identification of deficiencies in WCM, SCF solutions are presented as well as their main goals and key elements are determined. With a more profound understanding of SCF, the market segments and solutions are presented, resulting in a definition of an applicable SCF solution model that sets the platform for the analysis of market size and market potential.

The second part of the study identifies the global flows of trade that potentially benefit from SCF solutions. For this purpose, several company and commercial relationship characteristics are investigated with regard to their impact on SCF solutions. Finally, the potential SCF market size and the quantitative benefits for market participants are calculated and analyzed.

References

Bougheas S, Mateut S, Mizen P (2009) Corporate trade credit and inventories: new evidence of a trade-off from accounts payable and receivable. J Bank Finance 33(2):300–307

Croft J (2007) Supply chain finance utilised to save money financial services. *Financial Times*, 30.01.2007, p 18

Fairchild A (2005) Intelligent matching: integrating efficiencies in the financial supply chain. Supply Chain Manag Int J 10(4):244–248

Pugsley (2007) Global trade review, trade services and the supply chain, Sibos report

Richards VD, Laughlin EJ (1980) A cash conversion cycle approach to liquidity analysis. Financial Manag 9(1):32–38

Chapter 2
Relevance of WCM and Its Weaknesses

Abstract Working capital and the cash-to-cash cycle are important indicators to reveal supply chain efficiencies. Thereby, the objective is to balance and optimize the amount of working capital to successfully manage a company. Until recently traditional approaches were used to improve working capital mainly focusing on a single company. In contrast, the Supply Chain Finance approach provides opportunities to improve working capital for all parties involved in a supply chain.

Keywords Working capital management · Enterprise value · Accounts payables · Accounts receivables · Liquidity · Profitability · Cash-to-cash cycle · Prisoner's dilemma

2.1 Impact of Working Capital on Enterprise Value

From a shareholder perspective, a company's key focus is to make profits and thereby enhance its enterprise value. One long neglected lever for this, which has been arousing increased attention recently, is the management of a company's working capital (Bhalla 2005). Working capital can be described by the following equation:

$$\text{Working Capital} = \text{Current assets} - \text{Current liabilities} \qquad (2.1)$$

Working capital is one of the most important indicators of efficiency in a supply chain (Farris and Hutchison 2003). It is defined as current assets less current liabilities. Current in this context usually refers to a time horizon of a year or less (Emery and Finnerty 1997). Current assets are mainly made up of inventory, accounts receivable (A/Rs), marketable securities and cash and bank balances (Fig. 2.1).

Current liabilities contain accounts payable (A/P), notes payable, (current) accruals, as well as other current liabilities (Emery and Finnerty 1997). Hence, working capital is roughly the part of current assets that has to be financed with interest-bearing capital (Shin and Soenen 1998). A lower working capital can be achieved by reducing any of the three components of current assets i.e. cash,

E. Hofmann and O. Belin, *Supply Chain Finance Solutions*, SpringerBriefs in Business, DOI: 10.1007/978-3-642-17566-4_2, © Springer-Verlag Berlin Heidelberg 2011

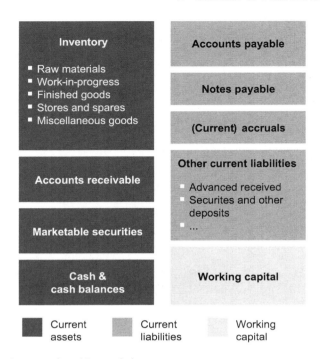

Fig. 2.1 The elements of working capital

inventory or A/R and increasing current liabilities. However, optimizing these components can have a direct or indirect impact on the bottom line (Scherr 1989).

Each company has to balance these components to obtain the optimum amount of working capital needed to run the business. The management of working capital aims at the minimization of capital tied up in a company's turnover process by reducing A/R and inventory, while extending A/P. These goals can generate several issues when looking at the whole supply chain of a company and a tradeoff between risk and profitability (Rafuse 1996):

- *Positive working capital* (holdings of A/R and inventory exceed A/P) strengthens liquidity since these current assets are easily convertible into cash. This mitigates risk, but harms overall profitability because of a large capital commitment, leading to higher inventory and financing costs.
- *Negative working capital* (holdings of A/P exceed A/R and inventory) leads to lower funding costs and thereby increases profitability, but bears risks and insufficiencies. A possible loss of production and supply shortage because of insufficient inventory might both harm growth and result in a loss of goodwill towards customers. Additionally, tighter liquidity might harm creditworthiness and hinder refinancing.

Considering the implications of both extremes, current research sets a low level of positive working capital as an optimum (Shulman and Cox 1985).

Fig. 2.2 The C2C cycle and
its components

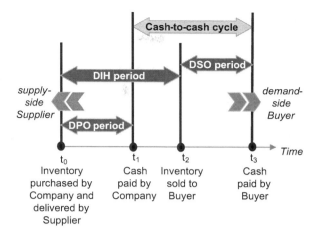

To optimize working capital, the cash-to-cash (C2C) cycle, introduced by Richards and Laughlin (1980), is an important indicator and measurement parameter. It indicates the time between the cash outlay and cash recovery of a company. The C2C cycle is calculated with the following formula (Farris and Hutchison 2003; Soenen 1993):

$$\text{C2C cycle} = \text{DSO period} + \text{DIH period} - \text{DPO period} \qquad (2.2)$$

- *Days sales outstanding* (DSO) = ø A/R/(net sales/365). The number of days that a company takes to collect payments from its customers.
- *Days inventory held* (DIH) = ø inventory/(net sales/365). The time in which the stock of raw materials, work in progress (WIP) and finished goods are converted into product sales.
- *Days payables outstanding* (DPO) = ø A/Ps/(net sales/365). The number of days it takes a company to pay its suppliers (Fig. 2.2).

Some evidence suggests a negative correlation between a company's C2C cycle and its enterprise value. According to observations, a 25% reduction in the C2C cycle of the average manufacturing company leads to an increase in the enterprise value of approximately 7.5% (Howorth and Westhead 2003; García-Teruel and Martínez-Solano 2007). Empirical studies confirm this observation and state a link between a shorter C2C cycle and a higher present value of net cash flows generated by assets (Shin and Soenen 1998). To calculate the increase in enterprise value, the discounted cash flow or the economic value added (EVA®)[1] model can be applied (Rappaport 1999) (Fig. 2.3).

As a company manages to shorten its C2C cycle, the release of originally locked up and idle capital increases free cash flow and thereby improves a

---

[1] "Economic Value Added" (EVA®) is a registered trademark of Stern Stewart & Co

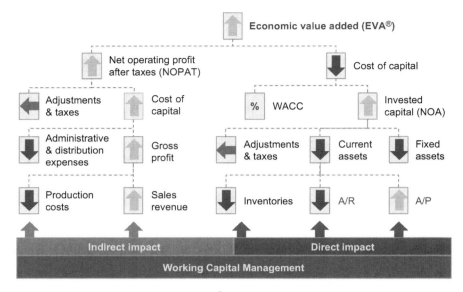

Fig. 2.3 The link between WCM and EVA®

company's internal funding ability, which facilitates sales revenue growth (Moss and Stine 1993). This increased capital efficiency brings about higher revenue generated per dollar invested in capital. Consequently, this enables lower costs of capital, which lead to higher returns on invested capital (direct impact) and increased operating income (indirect impact) because of lower production and operating expenses (Jose et al. 1996). A further impact is a better creditworthiness due to a greater perceived financial independence, leading to a better credit rating and lower weighted average costs of capital (WACC) (Hofmann et al. 2011).

The impact of working capital on enterprise value demonstrates the relevance of the approach (Hofmann and Locker 2009). However, practical applications have to deal with various deficiencies in WCM (Hofmann and Locker 2009).

2.2 Deficiencies in WCM

An enhanced view on the C2C cycle in Fig. 2.4 includes three sub-cycles: the purchase-to-pay cycle, concentrating on the sourcing and expenditure management on the supply side of a company; the forecast-to-fulfill cycle, which focuses on production, warehousing, forecasting and order processing activities; and the order-to-cash cycle, referring to the sales and revenue management on the demand side of a company.

Deficiencies in working capital can be identified according to the sub-cycles listed below (Reason 2005; Cheng et al. 2005; Callioni et al. 2005):

Fig. 2.4 The three sub-cycles of the C2C-cycle

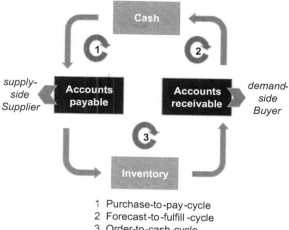

1 Purchase-to-pay-cycle
2 Forecast-to-fulfill-cycle
3 Order-to-cash-cycle

- *Deficiency in the purchase-to-pay cycle*: Problems on the supply side entail dealing with supplier interactions, cash disbursement, and DPO. On the one hand, buying firms want to develop long-term relationships with suppliers but, on the other hand, these vendors are often seen as a cheap source of cash. The result, when confronted with unanticipated volatile demand and extended terms of payment, is that a supplier's approach usually includes either an increased unit price or a reduced quality or service level in the long-term (Pike et al. 2005).
- *Deficiency in the forecast-to-fulfill cycle*: The cost of holding liquidity and material stocks can result in a lower rate of return of these assets because of the stock premium and, possibly, tax disadvantages. On the one hand, higher stocks reduce a firm's risk and increase its readiness to deliver. On the other, an excessive amount of cash and inventory does not maximize shareholder wealth. According to Ross et al. (2005), companies have to solve this tradeoff between the costs of cash/stock holdings (carrying costs) and the costs of out-of-stocks (shortage costs).
- *Deficiency in the order-to-cash cycle*: Delays in invoice reconciliation are a particular cause of additional working capital; they delay receipt of payments and increase DSO of receivables (Mian and Smith 1992). When there is a mismatch between invoice and shipping receipts, there is an inevitable delay while the imbalance is investigated. These reviews normally take time, as well as add cost (Pike et al. 2005). A typical tradeoff at the demand side exists between the gains from a faster cash collection, the increased cost of introducing and maintaining new debtor management processes and changed customer behavior (Reider and Heyler 2003).

Although those deficiencies can be dealt individually by a single company, this cannot be done at a supply chain level. The reasoning for this is straightforward when regarding two consecutive members of a supply chain. Any single organization in the supply chain has both A/P and A/R activities. Each invoice is an A/P from the downstream buyer's perspective and an A/R from the upstream seller's viewpoint.

Most companies require significant amounts of working capital to deal with variable and somewhat unpredictable financial inflows and outflows through their interaction with other supply chain participants. When viewed collaboratively, the challenges such as slow supply chain processing, unreliable and unpredictable cash flows, costly activities, high DSO and suboptimal credit decisions require a higher working capital than necessary (Hofmann and Kotzab 2010).

2.3 Traditional Methods for Improving Working Capital

To improve working capital, several single company-oriented procedural methods have previously been applied with the aim of attaining an optimum level of working capital (Ng et al. 1999; Farris and Hutchison 2003):

- *Enforced DPO extension*: Strong buyers use their bargaining power to enforce late payment to smaller, less powerful suppliers. Longer payment terms to suppliers are likely to worsen the commercial relationship as working capital is shifted up the supply chain, resulting in an unsound supplier base as suppliers are likely to have higher WACC.
- *Just-in-time and other inventory reduction solutions*: The consumption of old stock triggers new stock to be ordered in time, being directly available for production. However, since stock levels are determined by historical demand, any sudden unexpected demand rise depletes inventory faster than usual and might cause shortages and high transportation costs.
- *Enforced DSO reduction*: Strong suppliers use their bargaining power to force smaller, less powerful buyers to pay early. However, it can worsen the commercial relationship as working capital is shifted down the supply chain; buyers might face liquidity constraints because they have higher refinancing costs.

These traditional solutions tend to view working capital enhancement from a single perspective, either the buyer's attempt to defer payment/reduce payment size or the seller's attempt to accelerate cash collection—often pitting one side of the buy/sell transaction against the other.

Therefore, most companies focus only on their individual supply chain issues and take their own best interests into account rather than understanding the bigger picture and coordinating with their supply chain partners. As a result, they fall into the classic prisoner's dilemma (Flood 1952). The optimum solution to minimize capital exposure between buyers and sellers is to coordinate and cooperate, but because there is no coordination they work against each other and end up with a suboptimal solution.

Simply shifting the burden from one party to another can add significant risk to the supply chain, including customer loss, business continuity risk, supplier viability risk, material cost inflation, deteriorating support and a host of other issues. SCF provides an opportunity to collaborate and create benefits for each side of the transaction and improve working capital (PricewaterhouseCoopers 2009).

References

Bhalla VK (2005) Working capital management. Anmol Publications, New Delhi

Callioni G, de Montros X, Slagmulder R, van Wassenhove L, Wright L (2005) Inventory-driven costs. Harvard Bus Rev 83(3):135–140

Cheng NS, Cravens K, Lamminmaki D, Pike R (2005) Trade credit terms: asymmetric information and price discrimination evidence from three continents. J Bus Finance Account 32(5/6):1197–1236

Emery DR, Finnerty JD (1997) Corporate financial management, 2nd edn. Prentice Hall, Upper Saddle River

Farris MT II, Hutchison PD (2003) Measuring cash-to-cash performance. Int J Logist Manag 14(2):83–91

Flood M (1952) On game-learning theory and some decision-making experiments. RAND research paper

García-Teruel PJ, Martínez-Solano P (2007) Effects of working capital management on SME profitability. Int J Manag Finance 3(2):164–177

Hofmann E, Locker A (2009) Value-based performance measurement in supply chains - a case study from the packaging industry. In: Production Planning & Control 20(1):68–81

Hofmann E, Kotzab H (2010) A supply chain-oriented approach of working capital management. J Bus Logist (forthcoming) 31(2):305–330

Hofmann E, Maucher D, Piesker S, Richter S (2011) Ways out of the working capital trap: Empowering self-financing growth through modern supply management. Springer

Howorth C, Westhead P (2003) The focus of working capital management in UK small firms. Manag Account Res 14(2):94–111

Jose ML, Lancaster C, Stevens JL (1996) Corporate returns and cash conversion cycles. J Econ Finance 20(1):33–46

Mian SL, Smith CW (1992) Accounts receivable management policy: theory and evidence. J Finance 47(1):169–200

Moss JD, Stine B (1993) Cash conversion cycle and firm size: a study of retail firms. Manag Finance 19(8):25–38

Ng CH, Smith JK, Smith RL (1999) Evidence on the determinants of credit terms used in interfirm trade. J Finance 54(3):1109–1129

Pike R, Cheng NS, Cravens K, Lamminmaki D (2005) Trade credit terms: asymmetric information and price discrimination evidence from three continents. J Bus Finance Account 32(5):1197–1236

PricewaterhouseCoopers (2009) Demystifying supply chain finance—insights into the what, why, how, where and who. http://www.pwc.com/en_US/us/issues/surviving-the-financial-downturn/assets/supply_chain_finance.pdf. Accessed 09 Apr 2010

Rafuse ME (1996) Working capital management. An urgent need to refocus. Manag Decis 34(2):59–63

Rappaport A (1999) Shareholder value. Schäffer-Poeschel Verlag, Stuttgart

Reason T (2005) Capital ideas: the 2005 working capital survey. CFO Mag 21(12):88–92

Reider R, Heyler PB (2003) Analyzing sales for better cash flow management. J Corp Account Finance 15(1):15–25

Richards VD, Laughlin EJ (1980) A cash conversion cycle approach to liquidity analysis. Financial Manag 9(1):32–38

Ross SA, Westerfield RW, Jaffe J (2005) Corporate finance, 7th edn. McGraw-Hill, Boston

Scherr FC (1989) Modern working capital management—text and cases. Prentice-Hall, Englewood Cliffs

Shin H-H, Soenen L (1998) Efficiency of working capital management and corporate profitability. Financial Pract Educ 8(2):37–45

Shulman J, Cox R (1985) An integrative approach to working capital management. J Cash Manag 5(6):64–67

Soenen LA (1993) Cash conversion cycle and corporate profitability. J Cash Manag 13(4):53–58

Chapter 3
Characteristics of SCF

Abstract Supply Chain Finance (SCF) is becoming an increasingly popular approach in today's business. SCF is mainly driven by factors such as increased competition in the globalized market place, new technologies to process supply chain data, and the shift from letter of credit (L/C) to open account (O/A) in cross-border trading. At the center of Supply Chain Finance stands the inter-organizational management of working capital, the financial flows and the respective information exchanged across the supply chain.

Keywords Supply chain management · Working capital optimization · Open account trade · Automated collection solutions · Invoice reconciliation · Credit limit management · Compliance regulations

The meaning and developments of SCF have been analyzed from the relevant literature. As such, the development and differences towards traditionally applied methods are outlined as well as their overall contribution on working capital optimization. The environmental drivers and enablers that further impact the nature and potential of SCF solutions have also been analyzed.

3.1 Background

To understand today's working capital solutions—such as SCF—it is essential to understand the business environment of the pre-networked economy. In the post-war years, corporations did not think in terms of supply chains, but perceived themselves and their business partners as independent entities. Economic and competitive considerations finally forced companies to think in supply chain terms for manufacturing and delivering goods. As a result, the physical supply chain was born. Nevertheless, advanced concepts such as SCF went essentially unrecognized until more recently.

In many regards, managing large enterprises in the 1970s was easier than it is today. Consider first the duration of transactions. The time required to process transactions in the 1970s was long and arduous because the manufacturing supply chain itself was inefficient (Barovick 2007). Nevertheless, companies prospered, mainly because of the lack of global competition and, in part, because most regional companies were saddled with the same ineffective sourcing, distribution and lack of supply chain transparency. They did not solve the issues of their financial supply chain by linking the tasks associated with the information and financial flow from order placement to invoice payment.

Hence, those corporations with the most sophisticated and efficient material supply chains ever developed had little or no visibility into, for example, their receivables. That corresponded to delayed payments, inadequate working capital and high dilution rates. Today, these specific issues still trouble almost every global company irrespective of industry, size or region. Until SCF inefficiencies are solved, enterprises will continue to use an expensive hedging strategy against the uncertainty of financial flow and information.

Attempts to optimize SCF inefficiency are relatively recent. Core financial processes have long been automated, first through standalone accounting applications for the general ledger, A/R, A/P and inventory, and later through enterprise resource planning (ERP) solutions (Bougheas et al. 2009). However, they were never designed to function in a true financial supply chain. Therefore, solutions such as obtaining data from all trading partners resulting in higher transparency, providing automated reconciliation and injecting working capital into the supply chain were missing.

3.2 Relevant Supply Chain Flows

When approaching the topic of SCF, the general term "supply chain" first needs to be specified. A supply chain is a network of partners that supplies raw materials, assembles, manufactures products and then distributes them via single or multiple distribution channels to end customers. Along this supply chain, there are three parallel flows: goods and services, information and financial (Lambert and Pohlen 2001):

- *Flow of goods and services*: The flow encompasses services or products that move between the suppliers and buyers within the supply chain. Over past decades, there have been significant developments in making the processes involved in taking goods from the raw materials stage through production to the ultimate delivery to the end consumer more cost effective. By synchronizing the physical supply chain and aligning it with the flow of financial and information further efficiency gains can be realized.
- *Information flow*: Information associated with products and services as well as payments also flows through the supply chain. This includes purchase orders (POs), inventory documents, confirmations and invoices. This information initiates the physical flow of products and services as well as financial transactions. Up to now, information and financial flows were treated apart. Nevertheless, innovative payment solutions are now able to include detailed transaction information such as date and time of receipt of payment, quantity received and

PO number. By having both financial and detailed product information available electronically, an automated system can dramatically improve efficiency and establish a more tightly integrated supply chain.

- *Financial flow*: The financial flows in a supply chain consist of invoices, credit notes and payments. Financial flows in a typical supply chain encompass a multitude of invoices and payments between the market participants. The scale of this task is challenging companies to find ways of streamlining their financial flows.

These three elements co-exist where both the information and financial flows (the financial supply chain) support and underpin the products and services that move between the supplier and buyer (the physical supply chain) (Braun 2008). Traditionally, organizations have focused on improving efficiencies within the physical supply chain. However, the financial supply chain remained fragmented, complex and not integrated with the physical supply chain. Often, goods moved faster than money, and disparate parties were involved.

In the past, the amount of time required to process transactions was long because the financial supply chain was inefficient. Nonetheless, companies prospered, in part because of the lack of global competition and, in part, because all domestic companies were saddled with the same poor quality demand forecasting limitations, inefficient credit management and lack of supply chain visibility. They used the same strategy to compensate for these problems and hedge against uncertain demand, excess inventory, excess capacity and surplus labor. Since the cost of capital was low, reserve positions were routinely used. Not only was this "excess" strategy commonplace, it was considered smart management practice; inventory and A/R were considered attractive assets that "pumped up" the balance sheet.

3.3 Definition of SCF

"Ask the chief financial officer, the treasurer and the credit manager what SCF is and you will likely get myriad answers and opinions!" Similarly, if you ask a lender, risk taker or SCF service provider the same question, they too will have their own particular perspective on this subject.

For some, SCF is about managing working capital, whereas for others it is simply the flow of cash between corporations along the supply chain either in the form of a payment between a vendor and a buyer or in the form of finance. The latter can be either from a bank or a financial institution or from a supply chain partner willing to lend in the form of an early or extended payment (Robinson 2007).

However, this definition is too limited and needs to be extended to encompass the exchange of assets and liabilities within the entire supply chain. Therefore, besides cash and bank debt, SCF also includes A/P, A/R and inventory (Hofmann 2009).

Relevant literature describes SCF as the (monetary) reverse flow to the flow of goods within the field of Supply Chain Management (SCM; Presutti and

Mawhinney 2007; Lugli 2006). Furthermore, it defines three views on the financial supply chain: functional (company functions such as logistics, finance, investments and accounting), institutional (stakeholders of the financial supply chain) and financial (interrelation between relevant flow and holding parameters) (Hofmann 2005).

However, even this definition is a little too restrictive. At the center of SCF is the management of working capital and financial flows, but equally important is the management of the respective information across the supply chain and the documents and data involved that support these flows, such as POs, invoices and payment approval processes (Robinson 2007). Most of the information within these documents is that utilized to manage ever more complicated physical flows in the supply chain. The management of physical and financial supply chains around electronic information flows has been a key characteristic of SCF development in recent years. Enhanced transparency and visibility across both these chains has become a key ambition across the incrementally more intertwined subject of SCF.

In extension to these definitions, this study views SCF according to Fig. 3.1, namely that financial flows are in contrast to physical flows and their related information flows along the C2C cycle. Thus, the optimization of a company's SCF can be considered equivalent to working capital optimization. Summarized, SCF solutions can be characterized by the following key elements:

- *Dematerialization and automation*: The elimination of paper and automation are important prerequisites for the acceleration of financial and informational flow and timely solutions.
- *Transparency*: Transparency derives from the fact that automation assimilates a wealth of information by enabling internal and external sources to exchange data. Because of the better shared visibility of supply chain events, risk is

Fig. 3.1 The physical and financial supply chain

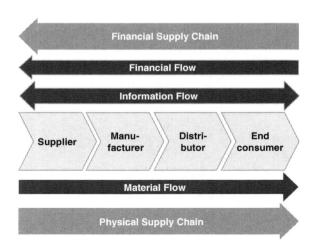

Fig. 3.2 Challenges of SCF

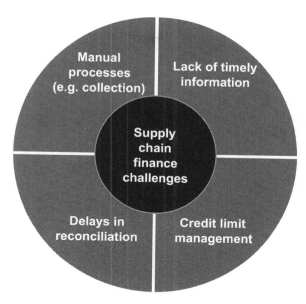

mitigated—since better forecasting and transparency creates certainty—as more information becomes available.

- *Predictability*: Whereas paper-based processes inhibit predictability, automation facilitates it by providing access to various sources of data.
- *Control*: Control is derived from the elements above: transparency and predictability are necessary to identify exceptions and confirm the actions, adequate control mechanisms and results that comply with both internal and external standards.
- *Collaboration*: The aim of inter-company optimization is to create trust-based win–win situations considering the end-to-end supply chain and stable trading relationships, as well as to encourage collaboration within the procurement, logistics, finance and treasury departments. Collaboration encourages companies to connect with internal and external partners within a supply chain.

3.4 Challenges within Financial Supply Chains

In today's market, companies require significant amounts of working capital to deal with variable and somewhat unpredictable financial in- and outflows. When viewed collectively, challenges within financial supply chains such as slow processing, unreliable and unpredictable cash flows, costly processes, high DSO and suboptimal credit decisions require higher working capital than necessary. If these challenges are removed, the money saved can be shifted to more valuable uses.

To strategically control and minimize these challenges and take appropriate actions, one must first identify and evaluate the common causes. The overview below lists the main challenges and related causes within the financial supply chain (Fig. 3.2).

3.4.1 Manual Collection Processes

In most cases, collectors rely on aging reports—bulky printouts of their portfolio of A/R—as the centerpiece of their recovery efforts. This collection process is paper-intensive and largely manual. Therefore, processes tend to be slow, unreliable, unpredictable and often more costly than automated solutions. In the meantime, the pace of commerce continues to accelerate, leaving credit departments hard pressed to keep up with the business volume (Jones 2008).

With automated collection solutions, productivity dramatically increases. In addition, automated services provide higher transparency, and clearly defined and standardized processes allow better monitoring of all collection activities, thereby realizing substantial performance gains in terms of DSO, decreases in past due balances and reductions in bad debt write-offs.

3.4.2 Lack of Timely Information

In many situations, financial flows do not contain sufficiently detailed information for either manual or automated systems to accomplish their jobs. As a result, additional time and effort is required to obtain the missing information (e.g. invoice-level detailed information such as ID numbers, item quantities and PO data) and the response time for cash flow calculations, reconciliation and payment defaults can be high (Gavirneni et al. 1999).

3.4.3 Delays in Invoice Reconciliation

Delays in invoice reconciliation are a particular cause of inadequate working capital within an organization. Insufficient reference details on incoming payments and unilateral deductions by customers are among the biggest issues corporations face with A/R, hindering them from automating their A/R reconciliation process. A typical A/R reconciliation process in any company consists of two distinctive steps: (i) reconciling the O/A A/R with the incoming remittance and (ii) reconciling the bank suspense account at the vendor with the bank statement from the bank (Min 2002).

When there is a three-way mismatch of invoice, PO and payment, there is an inevitable delay while it is investigated. Results show that collection errors take an average of four weeks to resolve once they have been identified. Most companies focus on large accounts or large past-due dates and do not devote enough time to other smaller accounts. As a result, many large companies lose literally millions of dollars each year from uncollected deductions.

3.4.4 Credit Limit Management

Companies mostly maintain their own departments to set customer credit limits. However, the ability to set optimal credit limits can require sophisticated algorithms that are often inaccessible to non-financial companies. By contrast, credit risk is generally not monitored or effectively understood by these corporations. Most suppliers do a poor job of gathering and analyzing buyer financial data, even on an annual basis. Automated processes, specialized applications and qualified professional credit staff provide better credit limit management, thereby shifting credit limits from buyers with low credit limit usage to buyers lacking credit capacity (Paul 2008).

In addition, most large corporations do not look enough at upcoming credit dilutions and payment default risks, particularly in fast-growing markets and buoyant economic conditions. They can and often argue that no default occurred in past years. However, this passive attitude suddenly changes once such a dilution event takes place. Dilution risk can be reduced considerably through higher transparency, fast response times and adequate credit management (Emery 1984).

3.4.5 Need for Action

Despite the fact that companies have made a large number of significant improvements within the management of their supply chain, there are still several challenges affecting financial efficiencies. Most companies are still using a Darwinian approach, that is the survival of the financially fittest supply chain actor. Why is it not possible to manage financial flows in the same way as flows of goods, namely in a collaborative manner? Notwithstanding the potential, relatively few companies utilize this approach as a tool to drive financial performance in a collaborative way (Simatupang and Sridharan 2005).

The introduction of SCF solutions tends to reduce and even overcome these challenges by improving efficiency, collaboration, transparency and introducing technology and external funding.

3.5 Drivers and Enablers of SCF

The need to overcome the main challenges in financial supply chains is underpinned by several factors. During recent years, these factors have been considered

Fig. 3.3 The enablers of
SCF solutions

key enablers that have resulted in the growth, availability and interest of SCF.
These driving forces in SCF should not be seen as separate factors but more as
dependent, interacting enablers (Fig. 3.3).

3.5.1 Globalization and Trade Growth

The globalization and decentralization of the supply chain have been the game
changers shaping the new ground rules of business. One of the main forces fostering this development is the outsourcing of capital intensive labor, production
and distribution to global partners down the value chain. The reduction of trade
barriers by bilateral trade agreements or World Trade Organization treaties has
facilitated global exchange as well. The growth of global trade has accelerated
strongly over recent years and is expected to continue at a similar rate. The total
world trade in goods and services (volume) grew by 83% from $2,093 billion in
1999 to $3,823 billion in 2008 (OECD 2009).

In a relatively short period of time, companies have transitioned from manu-
facturers to managing a complex network of third parties to supply, produce, store
and distribute their products and brands. The majority of capital is no longer
deployed to fund property, plants and equipment but rather to finance working
capital. Although the supply chain has lengthened as a result of globalization and
decentralization, many companies have experienced challenges in capital
availability.

All these developments come with the increased complexities, risks and costs
associated with a long distance supply chain (Carr and Gersper 2006; Merrill

Lynch and Capgemini 2007). To combat these growing supply chain risks, many organizations have begun focusing their efforts on minimizing the capital exposure in their supply chains.

3.5.2 Increased Competition

The world is getting smaller as economic boundaries dissipate to form a single global marketplace. There are several implications of this. On the supply side of the equation, more competition means price and margin pressure due to the increased commoditization of products and services with a growing number of substitutes and product varieties offered by non-traditional competitors. On the demand side, there is more variation in customer needs. The competitive mandate is to serve customers better, faster and at a lower cost. As a result, the performance bar for staying in the game has been moving up.

Owing to increased competition and little differentiation between vendors and their products there is an increasing demand in new ways such as extended payment terms for customers and reduced payment terms to suppliers increasing their market shares (Jones 2008). For instance, a buyer receiving extended payment terms from its suppliers will regard it as an incentive to purchase "products" from the respective vendor instead of products from competitors.

3.5.3 Supply Chain Management

Through SCM, which was developed in the early 1980s, companies better managed their supply chain through the improved collaboration of internal departments and external trading partners (Mentzer et al. 2001). The development of SCM resulted in a better management of a company's sourcing, procurement and logistics activities to meet customer demand, increase efficiency, reduce inventory and improve forecasting. Having experienced substantial improvements by applying SCM in the physical supply chain, companies are now turning their attentions to the financial supply chain to attain similar benefits (D'Avanzo et al. 2003; Otto and Kotzab 2003).

3.5.4 Change of Trade Paradigms

In recent years, there has been a strong shift from the use of the traditional documentary letter of credit (L/C) to O/A. According to estimates, the use of a L/C as a payment method has declined 20%, leaving more than 75% to O/A. Today, more than 80% of global trade is now in the form of O/A (Pike et al.

2005). Notwithstanding the security and financial flexibility of this trade finance instrument, L/Cs can involve high administrative costs, manual processes, expensive bank charges and high discrepancy rates, which add additional costs and time for the discrepancy process and manual matching. However, as companies move away from traditional trade instruments such as L/Cs, which provide some security of payment, they are finding themselves without the appropriate risk mitigation instruments against customer default. Today, the involved credit risk in terms of default and legal issues, especially in revolving trade flows, can be assumed by the SCF approach with appropriate services and trade finance instruments.

Global trade volume has doubled in the past decade and quadrupled in the past two. Today, more than 40% of companies worldwide trade with eight or more countries/regions and many trade with hundreds of individual market participants. One result of this explosive growth in global trade is a dramatic shift in transaction formats in the international trade marketplace, which affects both ends of the supply chain. Specifically, there has been a noticeable and ongoing transition from traditional L/Cs to O/A trade.

O/A trade has been proven to offer savings and enhanced efficiency throughout the purchasing cycle, particularly for companies with a one-to-many relationship between themselves and their overseas partners. Until recently, some rather daunting hurdles, including a lack of transparency and apprehension about cross-border exposure, had limited international O/A trade. Significant improvements in technology and an increased visibility within the financial supply chain, however, have minimized these concerns, making O/A trade not only manageable but also cost effective.

Today's buyers and sellers fully recognize the efficiency benefits of O/A trade, and they are moving quickly to make it the dominant payment method in their cross-border supply chain management. O/A is expected to become even more prevalent thanks to its ability to streamline processes by eliminating the multiple parties involved in the flows, while reducing the amount of documentation required in global trade transactions (Karako 2008).

3.5.5 Revenue Streams

Associated with a strong decline in the use of L/Cs, banks are losing a significant part of their international trade business (Juliano 2008). By looking for new business opportunities, financial institutions have started to adapt to an increased O/A environment and thereby support the rise of SCF solutions. They now engage in two main areas: the service area in which they can eliminate paper flow and provide straight-through processing (i.e. SWIFT solutions) and the finance area in which banks can fund necessary working capital.

3.5.6 Intensified Compliance Regulations

There has been a wave of regulations that affect the way companies deal with supplier and customer risk. Demand for greater efficiency and more control to comply with increasing regulatory requirements are the key focus of the regulations. Companies need to know who they are dealing with; although traditionally the focus of banks, this should also now be a priority for corporates.

Compliance authority regulations require companies introduce SCF solutions. The Sarbanes–Oxley (SOX) Act, for instance, has been especially important in forcing companies based in the US, and with listening on the Securities and Exchange Commission, to assess their exposures and gain a global view of collections (Carr and Gersper 2006). Under the SOX Act, A/R policies as well as reporting procedures are being scrutinized. This requires management to report on the effectiveness of the company's internal controls over financial risks. The act has elevated a receivables policy, procedures and transparency to a level of importance that might not have been considered fully before (Bouwman and Schuld 2007).

Hence, compliance acts provide numerous applications and triggers for the SCF approach. Regulatory requirements can be resolved and simplified through adequate SCF solutions.

3.5.7 New Enabling Technologies

By being the prerequisite for automation (speed) and transparency (visibility), new technologies, especially in IT and telecommunications, have paved the way for SCF.

Today, information flows such as invoices and payments are presented and sent electronically. Over one-third (36%) of European-based companies are already operating e-invoicing with either customers or suppliers according to a survey. In addition, digital signature and identification has become more and more standardized in global trade and has facilitated SCF (Schaeffer 2003).

Other technologies such as web-based applications and other interactive reporting tools are essential to successful implement a SCF program and provide the required transparency. They foster a better collaboration between suppliers and buyers, because improved communication enables the development of trust and more sustainable relationships. Hence, SCF processes can be greatly streamlined using reporting technologies, where vendors, buyers, lenders and risk takers can access the latest invoice status, check credit limits, payments and so on.

3.5.8 Summary

There are numerous drivers and enablers in the market environment that foster the application of SCF solutions and determine their nature. Although drivers such as international trade growth, the shift to O/A trade, a decline in banks' traditional business and compliance regulations increase the attractiveness to offer or apply SCF solutions, technological evolution is the main enabler.

The credit crunch starting in 2007 and the global financial crises in the following years decreased the potential for liquidity growth, and this has shifted attention from removing the costs, risks and embedded inefficiencies across an organization to improving cash efficiency, releasing excess working capital and enhancing enterprise value. The SCF approach helps to improve the required working capital in supply chains.

At a time when more products are sourced from emerging markets, which creates a more complicated and risky supply chain, and trade finance is increasingly being actioned on O/A, corporates need to consider their risk exposure as well as how to be more innovative in the way they deal with the supply chain.

References

Barovick R (2007) The new trade finance supply chain links money, technology, and more middle-market players. World Trade 20(9):20–21

Bougheas S, Mateut S, Mizen P (2009) Corporate trade credit and inventories: new evidence of a trade-off from accounts payable and receivable. J Bank Finance 33(2):300–307

Bouwman K, Schuld L (2007) Working capital management from a CFO's perspective. http://www.gtnews.com/article/6715.cfm. Accessed 12 Sept 2008

Braun A (2008) Corporate cash management trends—part 3: the financial supply chain. http://www.gtnews.com/feature/225_3.cfm. Accessed 12 Apr 2010

Carr R, Gersper MB (2006) Creating a competitive advantage in global trade. www.gdmllc.com/pdf/Competitve_Advantage_II_by_GDM.pdf. Accessed 09 Apr 2010

D'Avanzo R, Von Lewinski H, Van Wassenhove L (2003) The link between supply chain and financial performance. Supply Chain Manag Rev 7(11–12):40–47

Emery GW (1984) Measuring short-term liquidity. J Cash Manag 4(4):25–32

Gavirneni S, Kapuscinski R, Tayur S (1999) Value of information in capacitated supply chains. Manag Sci 45(1):16–24

Hofmann E (2005) Supply chain finance: some conceptual insights. In: Lasch R, Janker CG (eds) Logistik Management—Innovative Logistikkonzepte. Gabler-Verlag, Wiesbaden, pp 203–214

Hofmann E (2009) Inventory financing in supply chains - A logistics service provider-approach. In: International Journal of Physical Distribution & Logistics Management, 39(9):716–740

Jones S (2008) Corporate payments: opportunities for value-added services to be offered alongside payment products. J Paym Strategy Syst 2(4):392–399

Juliano D (2008) PrimeRevenue—creating innovative solutions for the financial supply chain. www.baft.org/content_folders/85th%20Annual%20Meeting/Juliano-The_Global_Supply_Chain.ppt. Accessed 09 Apr 2010

Karako KR (2008) Open account trade: how can cross-border companies benefit? www.gtnews.com/article/7193.cfm. Accessed 09 Apr 2010

Lambert DM, Pohlen TL (2001) Supply chain metrics. Int J Logist Manag 12(1):1–19

Lugli P (2006) Spotlight shifts to money in the supply chain. Financial Exec 22(9):54–55

Mentzer JT, DeWitt W, Keebler JS, Soonhoong M, Nix NW, Smith CD, Zacharia ZG (2001) Defining supply chain management. J Bus Logist 22(2):1–25

Merrill Lynch and Capgemini (2007) World wealth report 2007. Eleventh annual world wealth report for 2006. http://www.ml.com/media/79882.pdf. Accessed 09 Apr 2010

Min H (2002) Outsourcing freight bill auditing and payment services. Int J Logist Res Appl 5(2):197–211

OECD (2009) International trade and balance of payments. International trade world. http://stats. oecd.org/index.aspx?queryid=167. Accessed 09 Apr 2010

Otto A, Kotzab H (2003) Does supply chain management really pay? Six perspectives to measure the performance of managing a supply chain. Eur J Oper Res 144(2):306–320

Paul S (2008) A size-related issue?: Trade credit and the late payment problem: empirical evidence. Credit Management, Jan 2008: 26–31

Pike R, Cheng NS, Cravens K, Lamminmaki D (2005) Trade credit terms: asymmetric information and price discrimination evidence from three continents. J Bus Finance Account 32(5):1197–1236

Presutti WD Jr, Mawhinney JR (2007) The supply chain-finance link. Supply Chain Manag Rev 11(6):32–38

Robinson P (2007) The 2007 guide to financial supply-chain management. http://www.iaccm. com/loggedin/library/nonphp/Paul_Robinson_full_article.pdf. Accessed 09 Apr 2010

Schaeffer MS (2003) An 18-step blueprint to improve your company's use of e-invoicing, managing credit. Receiv Collect 3(9):203–214

Simatupang TM, Sridharan R (2005) An integrative framework for supply chain collaboration. Int J Logist Manag 16(2):257–274

Chapter 4
Segmentation of SCF Solutions

Abstract Supply Chain Finance solutions are segmented by analyzing geographic aspects, payment methods, different types of platforms, and the market players. A list covering several market players highlights the main funders, credit risk insurers and service providers for Supply Chain Finance solutions.

Keywords Supply chain finance solutions · Cross-border transactions · Domestic transactions · Payment methods · Market players · Letter of credit platforms · Open account platforms · Risk management systems

The SCF market can be segmented into geographic boundaries, payment methods, market players and platform types (Fig. 4.1).

4.1 Geographic Boundaries

Domestic transactions are commercial operations that are executed in the same country. By contrast, cross-border transactions involve corporations in at least two different countries with different jurisdictions. Domestic solutions are simpler because they operate in a single language environment and legal/regulatory jurisdiction, with usually only one payment format or infrastructure involved. International solutions, by contrast, are much more complex, with multiple challenges such as multiple currencies, different languages and multiple legal jurisdictions with distinct legislation affecting both procurers and suppliers. The lien of an A/R, for example, is a challenge because of the local laws and regulations in place in different countries (Mutter 2010).

In addition, cross-border transactions are more complex due to differing standards of domestic payment systems, the increase of international regulations and the changing landscape of emerging transnational and global systems.

Today, cross-border payments are slow, inefficient and costly for companies. The increase in global trade and improvements in physical supply chain efficiencies are creating demand for process improvements. Improvement in the efficiency and

Fig. 4.1 Segmentation
criteria of SCF solutions

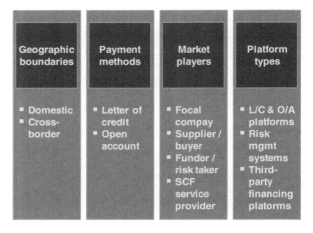

effectiveness of cross-border payments can be reached with adequate SCF solutions,
improved processes and systems in international trade finance.

4.2 Payment Methods

In cross-border trade finance, two main payment methods can be differentiated:
L/C and O/A payments.

4.2.1 Letter of Credit

A L/C, or documentary credit, is a letter from a bank guaranteeing a supplier that a
buyer's payment will be received on time and for the correct amount, if the
supplier presents it to the bank timely and in compliance with the L/C. Therefore,
it transfers credit risk from the buyer to its bank. In case of a buyer's non-payment,
the bank covers the full or remaining amount of the purchase. Payment under a
documentary L/C is based on documents, not on the terms of sale or the physical
condition of the goods (Mann and Gillette 2000).

The weakness of the L/C system is mainly the cost aspect because the
bureaucratic process can lead to suppliers being unable to perform within the
required time frame. Other problematic issues are high discrepancy rates with
presented documents as well as the cost-intensive administrative processes related
to manual document checking.

4.2.2 Open Account

Trade transactions can be also accomplished on an O/A basis. Under this approach,
the vendor ships the goods and expects the buyer to remit payment according to

the agreed terms. The exporter relies fully on the financial creditworthiness, integrity and reputation of the buyer. As might be expected, this method is used when the vendor and buyer have a great deal of trade experience with each other. Therefore, the O/A payment method is intended for trading parties who know and trust each other and are comfortable with the commercial and country risks associated with the transaction (Hudson and Zax 2007).

In foreign transactions, O/A can be a convenient method of payment if the buyer is well established, has a long and favorable payment record or has been thoroughly checked for creditworthiness. However, there are risks to O/A sales. The absence of documents and banking channels might make it difficult to pursue the legal enforcement of claims. The exporter might also have to pursue collection abroad, which can be difficult and costly. Another problem is that receivables can be harder to finance, since drafts or other evidence of indebtedness are unavailable.

4.3 Market Players

The market can be segmented into the different constituents within a financial supply chain (Fairchild 2005). These include a focal company at the center of the SCF solution, the suppliers and buyers of the focal company, the funder and risk taker providing liquidity and risk mitigation for the market participants and the service provider offering the required framework and platform for the setup of SCF solutions (Hofmann 2005) (Fig. 4.2).

Fig. 4.2 The market players of an SCF solution

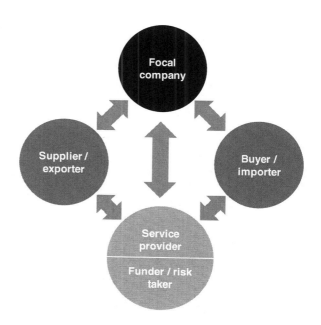

4.3.1 Focal Company

Focal companies are the primary drivers of SCF. They act both as an exporter (supplier) and an importer (buyer) of goods and services. Because SCF solutions require a certain size in terms of sales and volume to be efficient and profitable, focal companies are mostly large, multinational companies with international trade relationships (Fig. 4.3).

4.3.2 Suppliers and Buyers

These market players are always referred to in relation to the focal company as a supplier or buyer. Unlike in traditional WCM solutions they benefit from SCF arrangements through shorter payment terms on the supplier side and/or through extended credit limit facilities on the buyer side. Suppliers and buyers are mostly smaller than the focal company and are introduced to an SCF solution by the focal company.

4.3.3 Funders and Risk Takers

Financing institutions play the role of lender and risk taker in SCF solutions and offer various types of financing. Banks and risk takers can provide risk management services and offer risk mitigation in the area of country risk, liquidity risk, commodity risk, interest risk and foreign exchange.

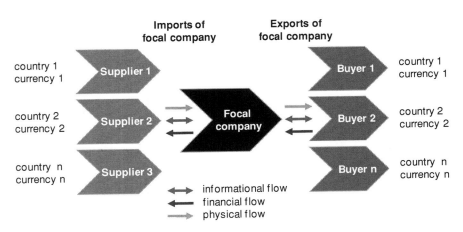

Fig. 4.3 The focal company as the starting point of an SCF solution

SCF is currently one of the fastest growing product categories for financial institutions in trade finance. Using new risk management methodologies that leverage the supply chain relationship between parties, banks are able to offer extended funding and risk mitigation to market participants in today's supply chains.

Below are summarized some of the main funders in today's market with details about their shareholders, target customers, partnerships and structure.

IBM Global Financing	
Headquarters	New York, USA
Structure	Limited company
Shareholders	Public
Target customers	Middle market, large multinationals
Customers	Nortel, Juniper, Lenovo, Advanced Micro Devices
Source	www.ibm.com/financing
Comments	Finance arm of IBM
GE Capital	
Headquarters	Fairfield, USA
Structure	Limited company
Shareholders	Public
Target customers	Middle market, large multinationals
Customers	Navistar International Corporation, Konica Minolta, Cisco, Delphi Corporation
Source	www.gecapital.com
Comments	Finance arm of General Electric
Siemens Financial Services	
Headquarters	Munich, Germany
Structure	Limited company
Shareholders	Public
Target customers	Middle market, large multinationals
Customers	No information available
Source	https://finance.siemens.com
Comments	Finance arm of Siemens
HSBC	
Headquarters	New York, USA
Shareholders	Public
Target customers	No information available
Customers	No information available
Source	www.hsbc.com

(continued)

(continued)

Citigroup	
Headquarters	New York, USA
Shareholders	Public
Target customers	No information available
Partnerships	Bolero, Orbian
Customers	No information available
Source	www.citi.com

Wells Fargo	
Headquarters	San Francisco, USA
Shareholders	Public
Target customers	No information available
Partnerships	Prime Revenue
Customers	The Toro Company, The Pep Boys
Source	www.wellsfargo.com

Santander	
Headquarters	Santander, Spain
Shareholders	Public
Target customers	No information available
Customers	No information available
Source	www.santander.com

RBS	
Headquarters	Edinburgh, England
Shareholders	Public
Target customers	No information available
Partnerships	Finacity, Prime Revenue
Customers	No information available
Source	www.rbs.co.uk

Next to the funders, some information on the main risk takers and credit insurers in the market is summarized below.

Coface	
Headquarters	Puteaux, France
Shareholders	Natexis Banques Populaires, Crédit Agricole
Target customers	No information available
Customers	No information available
Source	www.coface.com

(continued)

(continued)

Atradius	
Headquarters	Amsterdam, The Netherlands
Shareholders	Grupo Compañía Española de Crédito y Caución, S.L, Swiss Re, Deutsche Bank, Sal. Oppenheim
Target customers	No information available
Customers	No information available
Source	www.atradius.com

Euler Hermes	
Headquarters	Paris, France
Shareholders	Allianz, Swiss Re
Target customers	No information available
Customers	No information available
Source	www.eulerhermes.com

4.3.4 SCF Service Providers

Technology providers are the enablers of SCF. They offer platforms that connect all parties together and enable the visibility and communication required to support modern SCF strategies (Sadlovska 2007). Such SCF service providers facilitate the process of reconciliation, exchanging POs, invoices, credit notes, payments and related information as well as helping integrate this information between the different supply chain constituents. In addition, they can offer services such as credit risk management (CRM), the setup of SCF programs and the legal infrastructure for SCF participants. They bring various parties together such as funders, risk takers, buyers and vendors and understand the needs of each party (Gustin 2009).

Below are summarized some of the main SCF service providers in today's market with details about their shareholders, target customers, partnerships and structure.

Bolero	
Headquarters	London, UK
Focus	A/R, A/P
Structure	Limited company
Shareholders	SWIFT, Apax Partners, Baring Private Equity Partners, TT Club
Target customers	Large multinationals

(continued)

(continued)

Bolero	
Partnerships	Citi, Nordea, Fortis, Dresdner Bank, ING, RBS, Bank of Tokyo Mitsubishi, Bank of America, Zürcher Kantonal Bank, KBC, SEB, Dresdner Kleinwort, HSBC, West LB, Rabobank, Standard Chartered
Customers	Noble Group
Source	www.bolero.net
Comments	Open platform to enable paperless trading between buyers, sellers, logistics, banks, agencies and customs

Global Supply Chain Finance	
Headquarters	Zug, Switzerland
Focus	A/R, A/P
Structure	Limited company
Shareholders	Berggruen Holdings, Management
Target customers	Large multinationals
Partnerships	Deutsche Bank, Wachovia Bank
Customers	No information available
Source	www.gscf.com
Source	Founded as a spin-off from a business unit of a multinational food distributor.

Prime Revenue	
Headquarters	Atlanta, USA
Focus	A/P
Structure	Limited company
Shareholders	River Capital, RRE Ventures, Pegasys Inc, Battery Venture
Target customers	Large multinationals
Partnerships	Royal Bank of Scotland, Wells Fargo HSBC, Bank of America Merrill Lynch, Morgan Stanley, Macquarie Bank, Bank of Montreal, National City, Bank of America
Customers	Sainsbury's, The Toro Company, Pep Boys—Manny, Moe & Jack, Volvo, Big Lots
Source	www.primerevenue.com

Castle Pines Capital	
Headquarters	Englewood, USA
Focus	A/R
Structure	Limited company
Shareholders	No information available
Target customers	Large multinationals
Customers	Cisco
Source	www.castlepinescapital.com

(continued)

(continued)

Orbian	
Headquarters	Norwalk, USA
Focus	A/P
Structure	Limited company
Shareholders	Balderton Capital, John Kinghorn
Target customers	Large multinationals
Partnerships	Citi
Customers	No information available
Source	www2.orbian.com
Comments	Was conceived and developed as a joint venture between Citi and SAP

Finacity	
Headquarters	New York, USA
Focus	A/P
Structure	Limited company
Shareholders	Avenue Capital, Ecoban, Kleiner Perkins Caufield & Byers
Target customers	Middle market
Partnerships	RBS, Bank of America, Euler Hermes, Amroc Investments, Norddeutsche Landesbank
Customers	CHC Helicopter, Viméxico, S.A., Taenza, S.A., The Manitowoc Company, JohnsonDiversey, Cemex, ABB
Source	www.finacity.com
Comments	Specialize in securitization programs

Demica	
Headquarters	London, UK
Focus	A/R, Inventory
Structure	Limited company
Shareholders	J.M. Huber Corporation
Target customers	Large multinationals
Customers	Brake Bros, Smurfit Kappa Group
Source	www.demica.com
Comments	Company is a wholly owned subsidiary of the J.M. Huber Corporation, one of the largest privately held companies in the US

The Receivables Exchange	
Headquarters	New Orleans, USA
Focus	A/R
Structure	Limited company
Shareholders	Bain Capital, Redpoint Ventures, Prism Ventures
Target customers	Small And medium enterprises

(continued)

(continued)

The Receivables Exchange	
Customers	LAN Utilities Electric, Inc, TiaDel Secure Technologies, Inc., JCI Metal Products
Source	www.receivablesxchange.com
Comments	SCF services through an online auction for A/R

SCC Swiss Commercial Capital	
Headquarters	Zürich, Switzerland
Focus	A/R, A/P
Structure	Limited company
Shareholders	Zürcher Kantonalbank, Constellation, Management
Target customers	Large multinationals
Partnerships	Prime Revenue, GXS, Harland Financial Solutions
Customers	No information available
Source	www.swisscocap.com
Comments	Company specializes in sourcing, structuring and execution of cross-border trade finance programs for global manufacturers and regional distributors alike

Trade Card	
Headquarters	New York, USA
Focus	A/P
Structure	Limited company
Shareholders	Warburg Pincus
Target customers	Middle market, large multinationals
Customers	Brooks Sports, Burton Snowboards, C1rca Footwear, Dick's Sporting Goods & Under Armour, Hi-Tec Sports, International Playthings, Rasolli, Rite Aid, Wolverine World Wide, Abercrombie & Fitch, Guess, Levi's
Source	www.tradecard.com
Comments	Strong focus on consumer goods and apparel industry

4.4 Platform Types

SCF solutions mainly aim at facilitating and accelerating informational and financial flows within a supply chain. They can include different types of financing and payment arrangements between the supply chain partners. Below the most common types of SCF solutions in which a third party provides working capital enhancements to the different supply chain constituents are briefly presented.

4.4.1 L/C and O/A Platforms

L/C platforms aim at facilitating and accelerating the L/C process. Typical functions include electronic document preparation, automated compliance checking and credit management, which all aim to improve the overall L/C collaboration between focal company, suppliers, buyers and related banks. Consequently, some of the aforementioned weaknesses of the L/C process can be mitigated as costs are driven down, particularly because of lower discrepancy rates and less time expenditures.

An O/A platform supports a company's trade performed in an O/A environment by offering transparency, automation and decision support, usually being operated via banks or applied by companies directly. It incorporates functions such as electronic document presentment and the matching/reconciliation of payments and invoices, thereby streamlining and facilitating the transaction process. Owing to dematerialization it further provides enhanced invoice and payment status visibility for all involved trading partners.

4.4.2 Risk Management Systems

The main systems for risk management provided by service providers in the market include specialized CRM systems for SCF and transaction risk management (TRM) systems.

4.4.2.1 CRM Systems

As an extension to the decision support tools of O/A platforms, CRM services are also offered by banks, credit insurers or SCF service providers. These services include risk monitoring, collection of financials, risk assessment, rating and reporting. A CRM provider collects and filters relevant data from the focal company's suppliers and buyers to determine credit and supplier risk. This includes a quantitative and qualitative analysis of a company's financial strength, operational performance and business profile. The final credit risk evaluation might also take into consideration the flow of a company's electronic documents and cash movements (Felsenheimer et al. 2006).

4.4.2.2 TRM Systems

Transaction risk encompasses events such as supplier fraud, payment errors, overpayments, buyer insolvency during shipment and rejected goods. The management and tracking of the physical movement of cargo is critical. In this process, the TRM provider collects information about the physical movement of goods and then verifies, aggregates and analyzes the data. Therefore, various triggers are created, providing a better set of data to make solid underwriting decisions. Furthermore, trading partners benefit by these services because information transparency is increased (Gordy 2000).

4.4.3 Third Party Financing Platforms

This solution's approaches mainly focus on working capital optimization through C2C cycle reduction and risk mitigation (Jones 2008). The SCF solutions described below rely on the application of third party SCF solutions, which offer the important prerequisites of transparency (=risk mitigation) and automation (=accelerated data processing). This facilitates collaboration and enables triggers for third party financing at lower risk premiums (because of transparency) and at the right point in time (because of automation). In the following, the two main types of third party financing solutions are discussed in more detail.

4.4.3.1 Export Financing Platforms

In export financing solutions, the relevant focus is on A/R. The focal company (exporter) can convert its receivables before or immediately after shipment into the cash offered by a funder (Ling-yee and Ogunmokun 2001). The buyer pays the open invoices to the funder under their agreed terms. Depending if the receivable is based on a confirmed invoice, a bill of lading, a bill of exchange or promissory notes, the advanced amount or risk premium varies because its directly related to the outstanding risk. The invoice sale can be done both on a limited and non-recourse basis depending, for instance, on the vendor's buyer portfolio quality.

To illustrate how the SCF model works, the example below highlights the different processes involved and the role of the different parties in export financing solutions (Fig. 4.4).

Fig. 4.4 The export-oriented SCF solution (A/R)

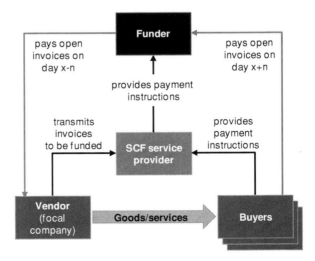

4.4.3.2 Import Financing Platforms

There might be different names used, such as supplier finance and reverse factoring, but this process is commonly referred to as import financing. With this solution the focus is on the A/P of the focal company, the importer (Berger and Udell 2002).

In an import financing arrangement, similar to an export financing solution, the vendor/supplier receives a percentage of the due payment up front from the funder and then receives the balance at a later date. However, unlike export finance solutions, the import finance arrangement is instigated by the supplier's buyer—usually a large retailer—through its own bank. By taking into account the buyer's stronger credit rating, the buyer's bank is able to offer to its supplier funding on more favorable terms. The bank is able to do this because the buyer's acceptance of the invoice is an intrinsic part of the import financing arrangement (Fig. 4.5).

The process begins with the buyer sending an approved A/P file to the selected SCF service provider. Once the file is uploaded, the vendor can access the SCF platform to view the approved buyer's invoices and decide whether to request early payment. If early payment is requested, the bank will review and approve the payment request and send the funds to the seller's bank account on behalf of the buyer. At invoice maturity date, if the vendor has sold the receivable, the buyer remits payment to the bank; if not, the buyer pays the seller directly.

4.4.3.3 Inventory Financing Platforms

Inventory financing platforms are a sub-form of asset-based financing, in which a lender loans money to a firm with the maximum amount of the loan linked to the

Fig. 4.5 The import-oriented SCF solution (A/P)

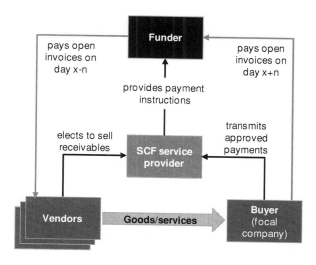

company's inventory. The range of money received from this type of collateralized lending is approximately 50–60% of inventory costs (Buzacott and Zhang 2004).

Because inventory financing provides the firm the ability to lend on its inventory, additional cash becomes available, which enables the exploitation of growth opportunities. Owing to their generally tight asset base, small and medium capitalized entities are especially likely to benefit from this solution. However, the amount of capital made available through inventory financing is very limited, resulting in confined benefits. In addition, the costs of this financing method are usually high, since the lender's possibility to monitor the underlying assets is constrained. Further investigations will focus on the financing of A/Rs and A/Ps in supply chains.

References

Berger AN, Udell GF (2002) Small business credit availability and relationship lending: the importance of bank organisational structure. Econ J 112(477):F32–F53

Buzacott JA, Zhang RQ (2004) Inventory management with asset-based financing. Manag Sci 50(9):1274–1292

Fairchild A (2005) Intelligent matching: integrating efficiencies in the financial supply chain. Supply Chain Manag Int J 10(4):244–248

Felsenheimer J, Gisdakis P, Zaiser M (2006) Active credit portfolio management: a practical guide to credit risk management strategies. Wiley, Weinheim

Gordy MB (2000) A comparative anatomy of credit risk models. J Bank Finance 24(1/2):119–149

Gustin D (2009) Supply chain finance: are we there yet? World Trade 22(9):14–19

Hofmann E (2005) Supply chain finance: some conceptual insights. In: Lasch R, Janker CG (eds) Logistik Management—Innovative Logistikkonzepte. Gabler-Verlag, Wiesbaden, pp 203–214

Hudson M, Zax I (2007) Open account trade and the changing nature of risk in the supply chain. http://www.gtnews.com/article/6727.cfm.. Accessed 22 Feb 2011

Jones S (2008) Corporate payments: opportunities for value-added services to be offered alongside payment products. J Paym Strategy Syst 2(4):392–399

Ling-yee L, Ogunmokun GO (2001) Effects of export financing resources and supply-chain skills on export competitive advantages: Implications for superior export performance. J World Bus 36(3):260–279

Mann RJ, Gillette CP (2000) The role of letters of credit in payment transactions. Mich Law Rev 98(8):2494–2536

Mutter (2010) The next generation of supply chain finance, gtnews. http://www.gtnews.com/article/7906.cfm. Accessed 22 Feb 2011

Sadlovska V (2007) Technology platforms for supply chain finance. Aberdeen Study, Boston

Chapter 5
Value Proposition of SCF

Abstract Supply Chain Finance solutions are accompanied by several quantitative and qualitative benefits, which are presented both for suppliers and buyers. These benefits are focused on a single company, but at the same time improve the efficiency and working capital of the supply chain as a whole.

Keywords Working capital · Liquidity · Credit risk · Transparency · Administrative costs · Reporting platforms · Supply chain relationships · Compliance

The implementation of comprehensive SCF solutions provides numerous benefits for companies in their supply chains. These benefits extend across the enterprise value of a company and at the same time augment the efficiency of the considered supply chain as a whole. A recent survey reported that for 45% of the companies asked SCF technology had helped improve their competitive advantage (Aberdeen Group 2008).

The value propositions resulting from SCF solutions can be separated into quantitative and qualitative benefits (Bernabucci 2007) (Fig. 5.1).

The quantitative benefits include:

- Funding, liquidity and working capital savings;
- Risk cost savings; and
- Administrative cost savings.

The qualitative benefits of SCF solutions include:

- Reporting benefits;
- Enhanced supply chain relationships; and
- Enhanced compliance worthiness.

5.1 Funding, Liquidity and Working Capital Savings

Inventory and A/R represent an investment in working capital funded through a combination of equity and debt. The cost of this funding can be measured via the

Fig. 5.1 The benefits of SCF solutions

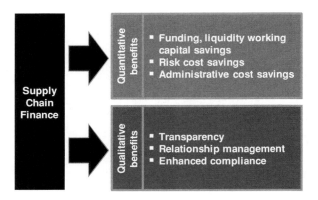

WACC. Through innovative SCF solutions assets can be isolated and funded at a cost significantly below either the company's WACC or the marginal cost of debt. The additional cash generated can be used by the company to repurchase expensive equity or debt, thereby reducing the overall WACC (Palliam 2005).

With an SCF solution a vendor can be paid "early" by a funder, whereas the buyer can pay the funder at a later stage. Payments will be received "clean," that is to say at face value and without deductions. The vendor is, therefore, no longer at the whim of customers' payment habits: payment will be received from the funder exactly when specified under the terms of the SCF program. This facilitates improved cash flow planning such that cash floats can be minimized and hedging costs can be reduced on, for example, foreign exchange exposure. In addition, SCF solutions have shown that excess working capital can be reduced as a result of the lower inventory requirements made possible through cleaner order flows and early dispute resolution.

For buyers, a SCF program also provides substantial benefits. Instead of increasing their liquidity through expensive and collateralized short-term bank financing they can receive any required working capital through increased credit limits within a SCF program. This provides a flexible pipeline of working capital with which to fund the cash cycle on a given product. These credit limits are generally accounted for as trade credits in comparison to short-term debts. Therefore, their leverage can be kept low and the company's credit rating can be protected.

5.2 Risk Cost Savings

Vendors operating in a global marketplace face several choices in dealing with customer credit risk (Tang 2006). They can request cash in advance (not ideal for boosting sales or maximizing supply chain flow) or use techniques such as L/Cs. As already described, companies are naturally moving more and more towards

O/A trading but here the choices for risk mitigation within an O/A environment are limited such as:

- *Self-insure*: The vendor takes the credit risk entirely on their own account. This requires a credit team of highly skilled credit staff but still exposes the vendor's balance sheet to potentially large losses.
- *Factoring*: Factoring on a "non-recourse" or "limited recourse" basis does provide risk mitigation but is expensive and is not a solution for large-scale, cross-border and fast-moving trade.
- *Credit insurance*: This solution has some benefits but does not provide a direct source of funding.

SCF solutions offer the advantage of O/A trading combined with the assurance of payment. Therefore, they provide a lower cost of credit risk than typical credit insurance premiums, or indeed the cost of risk borne by a vendor without any third party risk participation.

One of the main reasons for this is transparency. In most cases, SCF solutions provide the risk taker—which could be a bank or a credit insurer—with highly transparent views of financial and operational risks. This can encompass credit rating as well as the day-to-day operational and payment performances of the buyers, and provides a complete picture of the fundamental buyer risk, which is mostly not available today in trade finance, translating into overall lower risk premium costs and bottom line savings for the vendor.

5.3 Administrative Cost Savings

SCF solutions provide cost improvements on several administrative tasks within supply chain transactions such as reconciliation and credit limit management: With an automated system, reconciliation can be accomplished earlier, faster and at much lower cost.

Electronic means of improving the matching process for cash-to-invoice reconciliation have emerged and can perform a two-step matching process: firstly, on the payment from the funder to the vendor where all remittance details are provided to the vendor by the SCF system and secondly, upon receipt of the payment from the buyer, the cash is matched with the original invoice details and then notified to the funder accordingly.

When setting appropriate credit limits for buyers, a number of different factors come into play, including the financial performance and credit risk of the obligors. Monitoring credit limits dynamically and in real-time is difficult for vendors to accomplish by themselves. There are economic efficiencies in outsourcing the task of determining optimal credit limits and monitoring them dynamically. SCF service providers have specialized staff to assess credit risk and provide financial analysis as well as standardized credit limit management procedures. Because of economies of scale and dedicated systems, SCF service providers are able to provide this function in a more cost-effective manner.

5.4 Reporting Benefits

Reporting platforms commonly used in SCF solutions allow all participants access to real-time SCF information such as document flows (invoices, credit notes, etc.), cash flows and product delivery statuses as well as credit risk data and the payment behavior of buyers. Such reporting solutions contain sufficient detail to allow line item inquiries and provide enhanced transparency to all parties, thereby avoiding the need for constant manual intervention and dispute resolution.

SCF solutions not only benefit those directly involved in financial functions, but also provide in-depth analytical data for vendor sales and supplies, logistics and other process areas. Because information is provided through a web-based reporting platform, this can be accessed, for example, by sales people in the field making customer visits, enabling them to check on the sales volumes and credit standing of a customer before taking additional orders.

5.5 Enhancing Supply Chain Relationships

SCF can, in many cases, be viewed as an arbitrage: a company leverages its own balance sheet and volume to provide financing to its suppliers (free financing) at a lower cost than its own original standard credit terms, with the risk and servicing passed to a third party. The "free" financing that results for suppliers is a powerful competitive tool: to obtain the financing a supplier must simply supply products. This can have a compelling effect on interaction behavior and supply chain relationships (Simatupang and Sridharan 2005). For instance, a company selling a product that is not easily differentiated (e.g. raw materials) can use SCF solutions to differentiate itself from its main competitors. Therefore, a buyer considering two alternative sources of a product might be more predisposed to select the vendor offering extended payment terms.

Furthermore, increased transparency and shared information throughout SCF can further cement the relationship between the vendor and buyer. SCF solutions create a new customer relationship channel since they provide the tools and workflow necessary to identify and quickly resolve financial transaction discrepancies and disputes in a mutually agreeable, fact-based manner.

5.6 Enhanced Compliance Worthiness

With regulations such as the SOX Act the chain of command from sales to cash has to be mapped and analyzed as never before. Therefore, management needs to understand the effectiveness of internal controls on the sales ledger. However, this requires process mapping, identifying credit risks and the effectiveness of key collections, controls and reporting. Managing compliance with such regulations becomes easier if a company has more standardized and well-managed processes through SCF solutions.

5.7 Summary of Benefits for Supply Chain Constituents

This summary lists all the main benefits separately for the focal company and its suppliers and buyers.

Benefits for the focal company:

- Working capital improvement due to a reduction in DSO or extension of DPO, thereby reducing required debt and improving cash flow.
- Possibility of off-balance sheet funding.
- Mitigation of credit risks.
- Increased sales growth through liquidity injection into the supply chain.
- Lower operational costs because of automatic data processing, collection and reconciliation.
- Improved transparency for all related parties enables more accurate cash flow forecasting, finally enabling lower working capital holdings.
- Improved collaboration with suppliers and buyers through better communication between trading partners, which might reduce disputes over discrepancies.

Benefits for the suppliers or buyers of the focal company:

- Extended DPO or reduced DSO enabling off-balance sheet funding, which increases overall business opportunities, saves debt and improves credit rating.
- Automated invoice presentment solution allows viewing real-time information, monitoring invoice and payment status, enabling a more predictable cash flow.
- Increased transparency reduces any other costs associated with disputes or collection and payment processes.

References

Aberdeen Group (2008) Working capital optimization: finance and supply chain strategies for today's business environment. Aberdeen-Study, Boston

Bernabucci RJ (2007) Unlocking the value of supply chain finance. Bank Technol News 20(12):63

Palliam R (2005) Estimating the cost of capital: considerations for small business. J Risk Finance 6(4):335–340

Simatupang TM, Sridharan R (2005) An integrative framework for supply chain collaboration. Int J Logist Manag 16(2):257–274

Tang CS (2006) Perspectives in supply chain risk management. Int J Prod Econ 103(2):451–488

Chapter 6
The Market Size for SCF Solutions

Abstract Although there has been undertaken some research on the attractiveness of Supply Chain Finance solutions, little information is available concerning the market size. The study examines the potential for Supply Chain Finance solutions by looking at the different industries, commercial relationships, and company characteristics.

Keywords Supply chain finance solutions · Industry affiliation · Supply chain · Cost-benefit analysis · Trade flows

The analysis of the benefits to parties using SCF solutions in the previous section indicates their attractiveness and potential. A review of recent studies confirms this observation, but nevertheless also reveals that there have been few qualified attempts to estimate the overall size of the worldwide SCF market.

This study looks at which worldwide intercompany transactions benefit from SCF solutions. By looking for required company characteristics as well as identifying types and attributes of commercial relationships, relevant worldwide trade finance transactions are examined to calculate the market potential of SCF solutions.

The following SCF characteristics are further analyzed:

- Company characteristics;
- Commercial relationship characteristics; and
- Supply chain transaction characteristics.

6.1 Company Characteristics

To calculate the overall market size, company characteristics such as the relevant industry and corporate size affecting the potential for SCF solutions must first be analyzed.

6.1.1 Industry Affiliation

Industries that especially benefit from SCF are those that attach a high value to the main goal of SCF: to decrease the overall costs of capital by reducing working capital requirements. Research confirms this approach, since it was found that 56% of industry participants increasingly focus on SCF, mainly because of the general pressure to lower the cost of goods sold as well as the overall costs of capital in the supply chain (Enslow and Sadlovska 2006). But which industry characteristics are responsible for this pressure?

The strong need to lower costs is mainly caused by the goal to maximize enterprise value. On one hand, this pressure should be highest in industries with tight margins and strong competition. This presumption is in line with other observations stating that industries with significant concentrations achieve higher operating margins and returns on capital employed (McClements and Cranswick 2001). In addition, the need to lower trade finance costs is assumed to be most significant in industries characterized by above average C2C cycles.

To analyze the different industries and relevant indicators, the Standard International Trade Classification (SITC) is used, which is based on the ten product categories listed in Table 6.1. Each category represents a comparable industry.

To assign the potential of SCF to each industry, information about the degree of competition and margin pressure in the different industries is investigated. To employ this approach there is a special focus on an industry's level of consolidation because this is a relevant indicator of assumed market power, competition and margin pressure. At the same time, the duration of the industry's C2C cycles is considered to gain a second perspective on the SCF market potential.

Cash cycle indicators are obtained from a survey of the different industries in OECD countries (Hofmann 2010) as shown in the Annex. The competition indicators are calculated by using the Hirschman–Herfindahl index (Hirschman 1964), which is widely used to calculate concentration levels in different industries.

Table 6.1 Product and industry categories based on SITC	Product category
	Food (and live animals)
	Beverages and tobacco
	Crude materials (except fuels)
	Mineral fuels, lubricants and related materials
	Animal and vegetable oils, fats and waxes
	Chemicals and related products
	Manufactured goods
	Miscellaneous manufactured articles
	Machinery and transport equipment
	Commodities and transactions not classified elsewhere

- *Food, beverages and tobacco*: Food and beverage industries operate on relatively low margins because competition is high. Regarding the average C2C cycles, these industries have experienced an average of 62 days and 64 days respectively in the past 10 years. However, in the tobacco industry 118 days are the norm. Combining this information, there is an obvious need to reduce overall supply chain costs in these industries, wherefore an estimated 60% of the trade value could benefit from SCF solutions (Noble and Stern 1995).
- *Crude materials, minerals and mining*: The mining and crude materials industry is largely consolidated. For instance, in the raw materials sector such as nickel, aluminum and copper, five to six companies represent 50% of global market share. For global mining business, eight companies represent 75% of market capitalization. Similar accounts can be seen for mineral fuels. Overall, few crude materials experience a less consolidated market and high margins. A view on the C2C cycle duration in both industries reveals differing results. Although the mining and commodity industry has experienced an average of 90 days, the mineral fuels industry has only reported 35 days in the past decade. The overall potential for SCF solutions seems modest and should account for up to 30% in the mining and crude materials sector but less than 5% in the mineral fuels industry.
- *Chemicals*: It is difficult to get a clear picture about the degree of competition in the chemicals industry. Although the fine chemicals market is fragmented, the specialty chemicals market is more consolidated (Griesar 2007). Regarded jointly, the chemicals industry offers miscellaneous margins while being still fragmented with more consolidation lying ahead. The C2C cycle indicates an above average duration of 83 days. Therefore, the SCF potential can be seen to be up to 60%.
- *Manufacturing*: The manufacturing industry (manufactured goods and miscellaneous manufactured articles) is primarily characterized by a high degree of competition and low margins (Barnes et al. 2000). To increase margins, suppliers are often placed under pressure and production is outsourced. Additionally, an average C2C cycle duration of 97 days indicates much room for improvement. Both observations together give evidence for a great need to improve costs by optimizing working capital, resulting in an estimate of up to 90% application potential for SCF solutions.
- *Machinery and transport equipment*: The machinery and transport equipment industries are fragmented, but also include many niche market players with high market shares (Lynch 1999). The competition is increasing, however, as emerging markets place established ones under pressure. Considering the C2C cycle, a duration of 94 days is an average in this sector. As a result, an appraisal of up to 60% seems appropriate.
- *Animal and vegetable oils, fats, waxes and transactions not classified elsewhere*: The categories animal and vegetable oils, fats and waxes as well as transactions not classified elsewhere cannot be further specified since little information about competition, margin pressure or C2C cycle duration is obtainable. Hence, they are conservatively accounted for by a potential of less than 5%.

Table 6.2 Potentials of SCF solutions of different product categories

Product category (industry segment)	SCF potential (%)
Food (and live animals)	up to 60
Beverages and tobacco	up to 60
Crude materials (except fuels)	up to 10
Mineral fuels, lubricants and related materials	less than 5
Animal and vegetable oils, fats and waxes	less than 5
Chemicals and related products	up to 60
Manufactured goods	up to 90
Miscellaneous manufactured articles	up to 90
Machinery and transport equipment	up to 60
Commodities and transactions not classified elsewhere	less than 5

Based on research, the estimated SCF potential for each industry category is summarized in Table 6.2.

A review of the relevant literature indicates the potential for SCF solutions in comparable industries. In a recent SCF benchmark report, highest benefits were assigned to retail, manufacturing, electronics, food and beverage and pharmaceutical companies (Enslow and Sadlovska 2006). These results mainly comply with estimates made in this research study, which is taken as the basis for further analysis.

6.1.2 Size of the Company

To benefit from SCF solutions a minimum total transaction volume is required. The underlying assumption is that a company only considers adopting an SCF solution, if the generated benefits exceed the implementation and ongoing operational costs for its setup. The average implementation costs for SCF solutions are estimated to be $100,000. In addition, $10,000 annual operational costs on average have to be compensated (Koch 2009). Because SCF solutions are assumed to depreciate over 5 years (Nishimura and Venditti 2004), the relevant volume or turnover of a focal company has to yield sufficient SCF benefits to offset $30,000 per annum.

Regarding the size of the supplier or buyer, a minimum size is hard to set as their on-boarding costs to a focal company's solution model are assumed to be much smaller. The maximum costs implied could be the implementation of an electronic invoice presentment and processing system, although an inexpensive imaging system or an internet access for utilizing web data entry are also suitable solutions.

As already shown, a company's industry yields several constraints towards SCF application potential and a consideration of a focal company's size reveals the minimum required total transaction volume. However, there are several other characteristics that determine the potential of an SCF solution. Thus, as a next step, commercial relationship characteristics are considered.

6.2 Commercial Relationship Characteristics

To analyze the market size and potential benefits of SCF, commercial relationship characteristics such as the competition, risks and transactions in supply chains are determined.

6.2.1 Supply Chain Design

There are some constraints regarding the setup of a supply chain (design). A bilateral monopoly or restrictive monopsony, for instance, is a case of commercial relationships with only one supplier and one buyer. This limitation comes along with a low level of complexity because there are no large supplier or buyer networks, resulting in significantly lower benefit opportunities. Based on the calculated competition levels in OECD countries (OECD 2006), an estimated 10% of all supply chain designs are assumed not to meet the typical importer/exporter model as indicated in Figs. 4.4 and 4.5.

6.2.2 Supply Chain Risks

From the conclusion of a contract or the start of production to the after clearance process of a transaction, there are various trade-related risks a company is exposed to. These can be divided into four main supply chain risk categories. As shown in Fig. 6.1, these include country risks, exchange risks, transportation risks and commercial risks.

In the following, a closer look is taken at each of these supply chain risks by analyzing their impact on the trading relationship and eventual benefits/constraints to SCF solutions. Therefore, two scenarios are differentiated:

- The risk can be a constraint to the implementation of an SCF solution.
- The risk can be an additional (favorable) reason to implement an SCF model because the solution is a lever for risk mitigation.

Fig. 6.1 The relevant risk categories of an SCF solution

| Country risk | Exchange risk | Transport-ation risk | Commercial risk |

6.2.2.1 Country Risks

In contrast to domestic trade, country risks are a specific feature of international cross-border trade. These can be distinguished as economic risks, political risks or financial risks. In trade, especially the legal aspect of insufficient or missing invoice enforcement, is likely to have the greatest impact.

Sources of information for these risks are publicly available. The OECD rating published by the United Nations, for instance, distinguishes between eight country risk categories (OECD 2008). Since this risk is difficult to mitigate, the country risk of a transaction is unlikely to be reduced by an SCF solution. However, a high risk environment is a constraint for implementing an SCF solution because a stable and reliable trading relationship is required.

6.2.2.2 Exchange Risks

Exchange risk is present whenever a payment is received or purchase price is paid in a currency other than that in which a party normally accounts. The inherent risk describes the probability of deterioration in the exchange rate. To an importer this is an appreciation of foreign currency and from an exporter's perspective this is the depreciation of the foreign currency he is supposed to be paid in. As exchange risk is an external factor; it cannot be mitigated by the application of SCF solutions. However, currency risk should not be a constraint towards SCF solutions. The most common ways to reduce currency risks are various hedging techniques, which can be provided by financial institutions.

6.2.2.3 Transportation Risks

These risks encompass the possibility that cargo is damaged, lost or stolen while being stored or in transit. Transportation risks generally apply to the party who owns the goods, which can be—dependent on delivery terms—the importer, the exporter or a third party. A traditional way to mitigate transportation risk is through insurance (Global Business Intelligence 2007).

The inclusion of a transportation risk manager can benefit an SCF solution (UPS Capital 2006). A transportation risk manager provides SCF parties (the focal company and its suppliers/buyers) with detailed information about the physical movements of a good and its shipping status. Thus, transportation risks can be mitigated and triggers for SCF solutions are available.

6.2.2.4 Commercial Risks

These types of risks are caused by a company's commercial activities. They take into account that within a trade transaction either party (supplier/buyer) might not fulfill its obligations. The diversified nature of commercial risks makes it recommendable to divide them into sub-categories relevant to the exporter and the importer.

The *exporter's perspective* contains three main risk categories:

- *Production risks*: This risk takes place during the time of production before the goods are shipped and is related to events that might lead to the abandonment of production or omission of the good's shipment.
- *Risks of non-acceptance*: This risk describes the likelihood that the buyer does not accept the goods and thereby violates their contractual obligations (e.g. commercial disputes regarding the quality of goods).
- *Default risks*: The default or credit risk focuses on the distress that the buyer will not fulfill an exporter's payment claim either on time or in full.

One of the main commercial risks to the exporter is based on the buyer's insolvency risk and payment behavior. SCF solutions can mitigate insolvency risk through adequate information systems that provide payment behavior data as well as through credit insurance. Similarly, the buyer's payment behavior can be improved by SCF solutions as they foster a more collaborative and sustainable trading relationship. This initially intangible benefit should pay back in a more reliable buyer, thereby improving their payment attitude.

The *importer's perspective* consists two main risk categories:

- *Procurement risks*: These risks are composed of merchandise risks, the probability a supplier does not deliver the ordered good partially or at all, and quality risks, the likelihood that a good is not delivered in the contractually defined quality.
- *Insolvency risks*: If advance payments have to be made, the importer might also rely on a supplier's solvency in case of violated contractual terms regarding time and quality of delivery.

The risk of supplier insolvency can be mitigated through better internal funding ability, lower costs of capital or credit insurance. Procurement risks can be decreased by SCF solutions, resulting in improved collaborative and trust-based trading relationships.

6.2.2.5 Estimation of Supply Chain Risks

Considering the likely and hard-to-influence constraints implied by the different supply chain risk categories, we assume an overall deduction of 10% of the relevant trade volume within all possible commercial relationships.

6.2.3 Supply Chain Transaction Characteristics

For the ongoing analysis of the market size and potential benefits of SCF, characteristics of supply chain transactions are now considered. These characteristics can be distinguished as geographic scope, volume and frequency of transactions.

6.2.3.1 Geographic Scope

Geographic scope refers to the place of origin of trading partners. In this regard, the following distinctions are made:

- Cross-border ⇔ domestic trade.
- OECD ⇔ non-OECD trade.

This study focuses on cross-border trade between a focal company in an OECD country and its exporters/importers based in non-OECD countries. This distinction is made because of the high compliance of such trade relationships with the following key benefits generated from SCF solutions:

- *Collaboration*: A focus on a more intense collaboration is likely to have greater benefits, because the nature of OECD ⇔ non-OECD trade is characterized by relatively high risks and uncertainties. Liquidity constraints are more severe to non-OECD companies, thereby actions to foster stable and collaborative commercial relationships are often more important, since the focal company wants to have reliable business partners.
- *Transparency*: SCF solutions enable a higher transparency of financial, informational and physical flows. Although information is often relatively easy to access for trading partners in OECD countries, this is a far greater challenge concerning non-OECD trade. In this situation, SCF solutions enable the necessary visibility and high degree of transparency.

As a result, a focus on cross-border OECD ⇔ non-OECD trading partners seems justified since key elements of SCF solutions provide significant, above average benefits for these specified trading relationships. There is also market potential in intra-OECD or domestic trade, but the benefits are likely to be less significant. Therefore, this study will now focus on trade between an OECD focal company and non-OECD importer/exporter as shown in Fig. 6.2.

Fig. 6.2 The focus of the considered SCF solutions

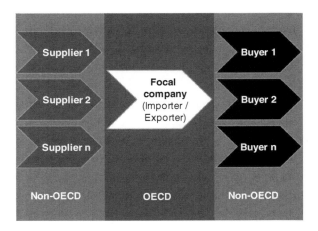

6.2.3.2 Frequency of Transactions

Similar to the determination of a minimum transaction volume, a relevant frequency of transactions between a focal company and a supplier/buyer is also more relevant to the former. To incorporate this consideration, a certain percentage of total OECD ⇔ non-OECD trade volumes is specified and deducted in the following, accounting for importers/exporters that have an insufficient frequency. For the following calculations a minimum of 120 single transactions annually are assumed as a minimum.

It can be assumed that most companies have regular export business. This presumption is based on the observation that industries with the earlier assigned SCF potential, such as food and beverages, chemicals or manufactured goods, obtain benefits by favoring regular transactions. Therefore, it is assumed that 75% of total trade volume fulfills the frequency criterion and happens on a regular basis (at least 120 times a year).

6.3 Cost–Benefit Analysis of SCF Solutions

In this section, a final step is undertaken to narrow down the previously constricted total transaction volume to its final SCF potential. To develop relevant import/export numbers and plug them into the SCF solution model, the benefit per US dollar transaction value has to be calculated to assess the savings potential for companies. Subsequently, this value is projected until it evens up the annual implementation costs of $30,000 as explained earlier, which is equivalent to a required minimum transaction volume. To conduct the benefit calculation, a theoretical transaction volume of $1 is inserted into the SCF solution model with all the relevant parameters.

6.3.1 Determination of the Relevant Parameters

To conduct a cost–benefit analysis, each relevant cost factor influenced by an SCF solution is considered at its level before and after implementation.

Therefore, the following parameters are specified (Fig. 6.3):

- With every transaction, a fixed level of administrative costs accrues. As an SCF solution is likely to have positive impacts on this type of cost, the original

Fig. 6.3 The parameters for the SCF cost–benefit analysis

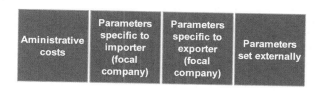

administrative costs without an SCF solution and reduced administrative costs after the implementation of an SCF solution are calculated. Hereafter, an average invoice value is used to assign the administrative costs to the total trade volume.

- Parameters such as DPO apply specifically to the importer. The DPO is considered before and after implementing an SCF solution. To calculate the cost savings experienced by the importer, the WACC is calculated.
- Accordingly, parameters specific to the exporter have to be accounted for. These are DSO before and after implementing an SCF solution and the exporter's WACC. In addition, the exporter also benefits from eliminated insolvency risk, and their dilution rate and savings in loss deduction are also analyzed.
- External parameters such as funding and the risk fee determined by the funder and risk taker as well the servicing fee demanded by the service provider are also considered.

6.3.1.1 Administrative Costs

The estimates of the administrative cost of a company's A/P and A/R process are considered fixed as per invoice. The administrative costs and the savings potential for A/P and A/R are calculated below. The main administrative costs related to A/P are inherent in the payment process. Table 6.3 provides an overview of the different cost estimates from different sources for the payment process without an SCF solution (Bass et al. 2002; Koch 2009).

Regarding the reduction potential by applying an SCF solution, there are also varying estimates. The results are listed in Table 6.4.

The average gives us $14.99 for payment costs without an SCF solution and $8.51 with an SCF solution, resulting in an average reduction of $6.48 or 43% per invoice. For the following calculation we assume an average payment cost per A/P invoice of $13 without and $7.80 with an SCF solution (=a reduction of $5.20 or 40%).

To determine the administrative A/R costs as comprehensibly as possible, we focus on a detailed cost analysis of the transportation industry (Bass et al. 2002). This leads to A/R-related administrative costs of $4.69. An overview of the original costs and the reduction potential by using an SCF solution are given in Table 6.5.

Table 6.3 Payment costs per invoice without an SCF solution

A/P payment costs per invoice without an SCF solution	Source
Approx. $11.60	Institute of Management and Administration, IOMA (2003)
Approx. $12.71	Institute of Management and Administration, IOMA (2006)
Approx. $20.65	Celent Communications (2008)

Table 6.4 Payment costs per invoice with an SCF solution

A/P payment costs per invoice with an SCF solution	Source
Approx. $6.81 or 41% savings	Institute of Management and Administration, IOMA (2003)
Approx. $8.64 or 32% savings	Institute of Management and Administration, IOMA (2006)
Approx. $10.09 or 51% savings	Celent Communications (2008)

As indicated in Table 6.5, the overall reduction in administrative A/R costs by using SCF solutions in the transportation sector is up to 85.5% from $4.69 to $0.68 per invoice. Other studies reveal 16 Swiss Francs (=approx. $15) per invoice for the consignor (=seller) and 20 Swiss Francs (=approx. $18.50) for the recipient (=buyer) without an SCF solution. Cost reduction potentials are seen from 30 to 70% (Koch 2009).

Since the values of Bass et al. (2002) are only typical for the transportation industry and are very low, we assume in the following average A/R costs of $14 without an SCF solution and $7 for the process with an SCF solution (a reduction of 50% per invoice). To assign total administrative costs for A/R and A/P, an average invoice value of $5,392 is used for the calculation. This average invoice value is based on an industry survey, presented in the Annex (Aberdeen Group 2007).

6.3.1.2 Parameters Specific to the Importer (Focal Company)

The parameters specific to the importer (focal company) include the DPO and WACC. There are various approximations about the average DPO of a company. According to research, the average DPO in all major industries was 50 days in 2005 (Hofmann 2010). An overview about the detailed average DPO in the different industries can be found in the Annex.

Other studies present similar industry figures of 51.6 and 48.5 days (Myers 2006; Reason 2005; Atradius Corporate Communications 2007). To generate

Table 6.5 A/R cost reduction per invoice by using an SCF solution in the transportation industry

Cost factor	A/R costs without an SCF solution	A/R costs with an SCF solution
Credit reviews	$0.21	$0.11
Paper costs	$0.15	$0.00
Collections	$1.28	$0.00
Payment application and invoice creation	$1.46	$0.28
Exception handling	$0.58	$0.29
Total	$4.69	$0.68

Source. Bass et al. (2002)

tangible benefits an importer aims to extend their DPO. An average DPO after the implementation of an SCF solution of 70 days is assumed, leading to a DPO extension of 20 days.

Another important factor for the cost–benefit analysis of an SCF solution is the WACC of the focal company, which is calculated by the following formula (Miles and Ezzell 1980):

$$\text{WACC} = k_e * (E/E + D) + k_d * (D/E + D) * (1 - \text{tax rate}) \quad (6.1)$$

where k_e = costs of equity capital, k_d = costs of debt, E = equity and D = debt.

In Table 6.6, the parameters for an exemplary OECD importer of German origin are listed, whose WACC is assumed to represent an average OECD importer.

Table 6.7 provides an overview of the WACC and its main components for selected industry sectors (New York Stern University 2010).

Taking into account these assumed parameters a WACC of 7.81% for the importer is obtained.

6.3.1.3 Parameters Specific to the Exporter (Focal Company)

The DSO carrying costs reflect the costs associated with financing each day of receivables, and depend on the number of days an invoice is financed (DSO) and the exporter's WACC.

Although the relevant WACC is assumed to be identical to the OECD importer's, the DSO ratio has to be derived differently. To determine an appropriate number of DSO, the results of a survey are consulted, assuming an average of 59 days in 2005 (Hofmann 2010). An overview about the detailed average DSO in the different industries can be found in the Annex.

Based on research, an average reduction of DSO from 59 to 20 days through the introduction of an SCF solution can be assumed. This leads to an average DSO reduction of 39 days. Further cost savings to the exporter are made on bad debt expenses, because these are carried by the funding or credit insurance party in an SCF solution. Although loss ratios differ within different companies and industries, a loss ratio of 0.3% is presumed. Additionally, relevant savings in loss deductions of 0.1% on average can be assumed for companies when introducing an SCF solution.

Table 6.6 Parameters for the WACC of a typical German focal company

Equity ratio	25.17%
Costs of equity (k_e)	12.54%
Market risk premium	6.80%
Risk free rate (10-year bond rate)	4.11%
Costs of debt (k_d) = EURIBOR (12 months) + funding spread	5.31% + 2.00%
Tax rate	15.00%

Table 6.7 WACC and components in selected industry sectors

Industry sector (selection)	N	Beta	Cost of equity (%)	Cost of debt (%)	Tax rate (%)	WACC (%)
Aerospace/defense	66	1.275	8.58	4.71	24.10	7.51
Air Transport	44	1.154	7.98	6.21	23.00	6.58
Apparel	53	1.140	7.91	6.21	17.21	7.06
Auto and truck	20	1.488	9.65	4.21	24.36	5.46
Auto parts	54	1.558	10.00	5.21	19.61	7.18
Beverage	41	0.949	6.95	5.21	16.46	6.54
Biotechnology	108	1.249	8.46	6.21	3.59	8.23
Building materials	52	1.391	9.16	6.21	18.44	7.08
Chemical (diversified)	33	1.213	8.28	4.71	25.47	7.27
Chemical (speciality)	88	1.185	8.13	6.21	18.99	7.32
Computer software	322	1.223	8.33	6.21	12.65	8.12
Computers/peripherals	125	1.295	8.68	6.21	9.90	8.21
Drug	342	1.162	8.02	6.21	5.96	7.74
E-commerce	54	1.497	9.70	5.21	13.09	9.17
Electric util.	24	0.823	6.32	3.21	33.02	4.16
Electrical equipment	83	1.373	9.07	5.21	14.23	8.20
Electronics	173	1.312	8.77	6.21	11.87	7.74
Food processing	109	0.798	6.20	4.71	21.67	5.55
Food wholesalers	18	0.727	5.84	4.71	27.39	4.94
Home furnishings	34	1.293	8.68	4.71	23.99	6.65
Grocery	14	0.838	6.40	3.71	32.96	5.92
Household products	26	1.080	7.61	4.21	29.87	6.73
Industrial services	167	1.197	8.20	6.21	19.26	7.22
Machinery	124	1.390	9.16	5.21	22.71	7.32
Maritime	56	1.305	8.73	6.21	7.08	6.81
Medical supplies	252	1.167	8.04	6.21	12.51	7.74
Metal fabricating	35	1.556	9.99	6.21	20.43	8.96
Metals and mining (div.)	78	1.686	10.64	6.21	9.29	9.74
Natural gas utility	25	0.692	5.67	3.71	24.52	4.35
Office equip/supplies	26	1.111	7.76	4.71	22.76	6.21
Oil/gas distribution	19	0.894	6.68	4.71	9.48	5.59
Oilfield services/equip.	112	1.557	9.99	4.71	22.07	8.11
Packaging and container	33	1.265	8.54	4.71	24.65	6.25
Paper/forest products	38	1.205	8.23	5.21	13.66	6.21
Petroleum (producing)	188	1.242	8.42	6.21	13.98	7.58
Power	66	1.630	10.36	6.21	6.25	8.00
Precious metals	75	1.415	9.28	6.21	5.94	8.92
Precision instrument	90	1.466	9.54	6.21	14.38	8.76
Restaurant	68	1.260	8.51	5.21	20.10	7.64
Retail automotive	16	1.313	8.78	4.21	34.23	6.37

(continued)

Table 6.7 (continued)

Industry sector (selection)	N	Beta	Cost of equity (%)	Cost of debt (%)	Tax rate (%)	WACC (%)
Retail store	38	1.006	7.24	4.71	25.68	6.37
Semiconductor	122	1.809	11.25	6.21	10.48	10.59
Semiconductor equip	16	1.777	11.10	4.71	22.03	10.21
Steel (general)	20	1.713	10.77	4.71	29.15	8.96
Telecom. equipment	110	1.488	9.65	6.21	12.08	9.18
Telecom. services	140	1.426	9.34	6.21	15.90	7.94
Tobacco	12	0.713	5.77	6.21	20.25	5.71
Trucking	33	1.167	8.05	4.71	33.19	5.31
Wireless networking	57	1.538	9.90	6.21	14.08	8.68

6.3.1.4 Parameters Set Externally

To estimate the benefits of SCF solutions for both the focal company and the importer/exporter, several external parameters are considered. These parameters include the funding, credit risk and servicing fee from third parties:

- *Funder*: The funding fee is generally calculated as a base rate (e.g. London Interbank Offered Rate (LIBOR) plus a funding spread). Although the LIBOR is determined by the market, the funding spread represents the bank's funding margin. An average funding spread of 3% based on the balance of funds in use is assumed for this research (New York Stern University 2008b).
- *Risk taker*: Usually a credit risk premium for risk cover of up to 90% on any buyer default has to be paid by the importer. The pricing of the risk fee is generally based on elements such as credit size, diversification, country and credit rating as well as the concentrations of the debtors. Based on experience a realistic risk fee is 0.2% annually on trading volume. Other calculation models use outstandings, credit limits or other factors as underlying parameters.
- *Service provider*: The servicing fee of the service provider for implementing and maintaining the SCF platform as well as servicing the overall SCF program is usually around 0.3% of the transaction (processing) volume.
- *Non-OECD supplier/buyer*: The benefits for the focal company's suppliers and buyers depend significantly on their WACC. Because no reliable information is available about average equity ratios, beta values or funding spreads for an average non-OECD company, their WACC is estimated to be 15% (New York Stern University 2008a).

Having defined all parameter values, a cost–benefit analysis can be applied to calculate the required minimum transaction volume for SCF solutions to break even. In the following, the benefit calculations for the importer and exporter are presented in detail.

6.3.2 Cost–Benefit Analysis to the Importer

The benefit is calculated by using a theoretical A/P amount of $1 in the formula in Table 6.8. The calculation results in a net benefit for every A/P dollar of $0.0089. If it is assumed that it costs $30,000 annually to implement an SCF solution model, purchases of $3,373,984 from non-OECD companies are required to offset the implementation costs. Although this minimum purchasing volume does not quantify the exact potential savings number, it can be derived that net savings are generated from a relevant purchasing amount greater than $3,373,984. If this level is achieved, potential savings are $0.0082 multiplied by additionally relevant A/P.

> An importing focal company generates potential savings by implementing an SCF solution if its non-OECD purchase volume is greater than $3,373,984. Additional purchases yield savings of $0.0089 per US dollar.

To quantify the impact of this required amount on SCF solutions, it is estimated that, after all other constraining criteria have been applied, up to 75% of the remaining total import volume per annum from non-OECD companies is likely to be in the range of $3,373,984 or bigger.

6.3.3 Cost–Benefit Analysis to the Exporter

Below the costs–benefit analysis calculation for the exporter is presented.

To calculate the net benefits for an exporter, a theoretical A/R value of $1 is applied. Transferring this value to the formula in Table 6.9 results in a net benefit of $0.016 for every A/R dollar. To outweigh the implementation costs of

Table 6.8 Calculation of the net benefit of an SCF solution to an importer

Unlocked working capital	Importer's WACC * ((DPO of importer without an SCF solution *less* DPO of importer with an SCF solution)/365) * A/P
+ Administration benefit	Total administration costs without an SCF solution *less* total administration costs with an SCF solution = saving per invoice payable* (A/P/average invoice value)
− Funding fee	Funding fee * ((DPO of importer without an SCF solution *less* DPO of importer with an SCF solution)/365) * A/P
− Servicing fee	Servicing fee * ((DPO of importer without an SCF solution *less* DPO of importer with an SCF solution)/365) * A/P
= Net benefit	Tangible net benefit to the importer by implementing an SCF solution

Table 6.9 Calculation of the net benefit of an SCF solution to an exporter

Risk benefit	Loss ratio * A/R
+ Unlocked working capital	Exporter's WACC * (DSO reduction/365) * A/R
+ Administration benefit	Administration costs without an SCF solution *less* administration costs with an SCF solution = saving per invoice receivable * (A/R/average invoice value)
+ Savings in loss deduction	Savings in loss deduction rate * A/R
− Funding fee	Funding fee * (DSO reduction/365) * A/R
− Risk fee	Annual risk fee * ((credit period to buyers/365) * A/R)
− Servicing fee	Servicing fee * (DSO reduction/365) * A/R
= Net benefit	Tangible net benefit to the exporter by implementing an SCF solution

$30,000 annually, a relevant turnover from non-OECD buyers of $1,904,937 is required. Similar to the importer's case, this volume of relevant turnover does not quantify the exact potential savings number. However, it can be stated that net savings are achieved if the non-OECD turnover volume is greater than $1,904,937. As an implication, a contribution to overall savings is made from every excess A/R dollar in the amount of $0.016 multiplied by the additionally relevant A/R.

> An exporting focal company generates potential savings by implementing an SCF solution if its non-OECD turnover volume is greater than $1,904,937. Additional turnover yields savings of $0.016 per US dollar.

Since the net benefit to the exporter is similar to the importer, it is likely that its impact on SCF application is also in the same range. Thus, after all other constraining criteria have been applied, 75% of the remaining total exports to non-OECD companies are considered in the range of $1,904,937 per annum or bigger.

It should be noted, however, that the actual required volume might be lower since there are many intangible benefits such as collaboration and transparency that have not been considered. These benefits could further increase the value proposition of SCF solutions.

6.4 Application of the SCF Model

Up to this point, company and transaction characteristics have been analyzed and constraints in the overall potential of SCF solutions have been identified. As a next step, the developed limitations are adopted to a total number of imports/exports, resulting in relevant amounts of A/P and A/R (OECD 2006).

6.4.1 Estimation of Relevant Trade Flows

To calculate the relevant imports and exports, as indicated in the following tables, total flows of trade are extracted from the OECD's statistical database for every product/industry category. An overview of the detailed flows of trade related to each OECD country can be found in the Annex. Subsequently, trade flow numbers are narrowed down and the total amount of imports/exports that benefiting from SCF solutions is obtained. Table 6.10 presents the relevant imports from non-OECD countries.

As can be inferred from Table 6.10, the constraints overall reduce the SCF application potential from $2,770,260 million to $702,843 million, which accounts for approximately 25%. Table 6.11 displays the adoption of limitations to non-OECD exports.

The SCF potential from non-OECD directed imports is estimated at $702,843 million. The potential for directed exports is estimated at $547,049 million.

Table 6.11 reveals that the SCF potential to non-OECD directed exports is only reduced by approximately 30% from $1,802,899 to $547,049 million. The 5% difference in application potential compared with the import figures can be explained by the different weighting of product categories.

As the developed limitations of the SCF solution are incorporated and import and export trade numbers are adjusted, the full SCF calculation model is established in the next section.

6.4.2 Tangible Benefits of an SCF Solution

So far, the method for conducting a cost–benefit analysis regarding the implementation of SCF solutions has been solely introduced for a focal company. To obtain a complete picture of the tangible benefits for all supply chain constituents, the residual formulas for supplier and buyer are used, as shown below. They are separated into cash flows originated in an SCF import and export model.

Table 6.10 Application of SCF limitations to non-OECD imports in 2006

Product (industry) category	All imports from non-OECD suppliers (in m)	Industry constraints	Risk constraints	Frequency criteria	Volume constraints
Food (and live animals)	$130,379	60%	90%	75%	75%
Beverages and tobacco	$7,340	60%	90%	75%	75%
Crude materials	$107,395	30%	90%	75%	75%
Mineral fuels, lubricants and related materials	$753,134	5%	90%	75%	75%
Animal and vegetable oils, fats and waxes	$9,771	5%	90%	75%	75%
Chemicals and related products	$114,069	60%	90%	75%	75%
Manufactured goods	$357,509	90%	90%	75%	75%
Miscellaneous manufactured articles	$473,946	90%	90%	75%	75%
Machinery and transport equipment	$725,870	60%	90%	75%	75%
Commodities and transactions not classified	$90,847	5%	90%	75%	75%
Total imports (in m)	$2,770,260	$1,388,331	$1,249,498	$937,123	$702,843

Table 6.11 Application of SCF limitations to non-OECD exports in 2006

Product (industry) category	All exports to non-OECD buyers (in m)	Industry constraints	Risk constraints	Frequency criteria	Volume constraints
Food (and live animals)	$73,030	60%	90%	75%	75%
Beverages and tobacco	$11,388	60%	90%	75%	75%
Crude materials	$70,265	30%	90%	75%	75%
Mineral fuels, lubricants and related materials	$74,260	5%	90%	75%	75%
Animal and vegetable oils, fats and waxes	$2,829	5%	90%	75%	75%
Chemicals and related products	$207,493	60%	90%	75%	75%
Manufactured goods	$252,267	90%	90%	75%	75%
Miscellaneous manufactured articles	$158,044	90%	90%	75%	75%
Machinery and transport equipment	$868,396	60%	90%	75%	75%
Commodities and transactions not classified	$84,925	5%	90%	75%	75%
Total exports (in m)	$1,802,899	$1,080,591	$972,532	$729,399	$547,049

Table 6.12 Tangible net benefit to suppliers in the SCF importer model

Unlocked working capital	Supplier's WACC * (granted credit period to supplier/365) * A/P
− Funding Fee	Funding fee * (granted credit period to supplier/365) * A/P
= Tangible net benefit	Tangible net benefit to the supplier by implementing an SCF solution

6.4.2.1 Benefits to Suppliers in the SCF Importer Model

In the import model, tangible benefits to suppliers are calculated according to the formulas in Table 6.12.

6.4.2.2 Benefits to Buyers in the SCF Exporter Model

The calculations of the tangible benefits to buyers (=customers of the exporting focal company) are presented in Table 6.13.

In the following steps, these derived parameter values are inserted into the formulas.

6.4.3 Import SCF Model

The relevant parameters previously indicated for the import supply chain model are summarized in Table 6.14.

By inserting the parameter values into the formulas we presented earlier, the net benefits and revenue streams to the focal company (importer) and its suppliers are calculated, as listed in Table 6.15.

6.4.4 Export SCF Model

To gain a better understanding of the calculated tangible benefits to SCF parties in the export model, the relevant parameters previously indicated are displayed in Table 6.16.

Table 6.13 Tangible net benefit to buyers in the SCF exporter model

Unlocked working capital	Buyer's WACC * (granted credit period to the buyer/365) * A/R
− Funding Fee	Funding fee * (granted credit period to the buyer/365) * A/R
= Tangible net benefit	Tangible net benefit to the buyer by implementing an SCF solution

Table 6.14 Overview of relevant parameter values in the SCF import model

Annual A/P	$702,843,000
DPO of focal company (importer) without an SCF solution	50 days
DPO of focal company (importer) with an SCF solution	70 days
DSO of suppliers without an SCF solution	59 days
DSO of suppliers with an SCF solution	20 days
Funding fee	3.00%
Risk fee	0.20%
Servicing fee	0.30%
WACC of focal company (OECD) [importer]	7.81%
WACC of supplier (non-OECD)	15.00%
Average number of invoices	810
Process cost per invoice payable without an SCF solution	$13
Process cost per invoice payable with an SCF solution	$7.80

Table 6.15 Net benefits and revenue streams to SCF parties in the import model

Focal company (importer)	
Unlocked working capital (in m)	$3.008
+ Administration benefit (in m)	$4.512
− Financing costs (in m)	$1.155
− Servicing costs (in m)	$0.115
= Net benefit (in m)	$6.249
Supplier	
Unlocked working capital (in m)	$11.265
− Financing costs (in m)	$2.253
= Net benefit (in m)	$9.012

Table 6.16 Overview of relevant parameter values in the SCF export model

Annual A/R	$554,164,000
DSO of focal company (exporter) without an SCF solution	59 days
DSO of focal company (exporter) with an SCF solution	20 days
DPO of the buyers without an SCF solution	50 days
DPO of buyers with an SCF solution	70 days
Funding fee	3.00%
Risk fee	0.20%
Servicing fee	0.30%
Dilution rate (loss ratio)	0.30%
Savings in loss deduction	0.10%
WACC of focal company (OECD) [exporter]	7.81%
WACC of buyer (non-OECD)	15.00%
Average number of invoices	810
Process cost per invoice receivable without an SCF solution	$14
Process cost per invoice receivable with an SCF solution	$7

Table 6.17 Net benefits and revenue streams to SCF parties in the export model

Focal company (exporter)	
Unlocked working capital (in m)	$4.565
+ Administration benefit (in m)	$4.728
+ Risk benefit (in m)	$1.641
+ Savings in loss deduction (in m)	$547
− Financing costs (in m)	$1.754
− Risk costs (in m)	$0.060
− Servicing costs (in m)	$0.175
= Net benefit (in m)	$9.492
Buyer	
Unlocked working capital (in m)	$4.496
− Financing costs (in m)	$0.899
= Net benefit (in m)	$3.597

To obtain the net benefits and revenue streams to SCF parties in the export model according to Table 6.17, parameter values are inserted into the respective formulas.

6.5 Summary of Results

The results of the different calculations of the different SCF solutions are summarized below:

- The potential market size for SCF solutions for non-OECD directed imports is estimated to be $702,843 million.
- The potential market size for SCF solutions for non-OECD directed exports is estimated to be $547,049 million.
- An importing focal company generates potential savings by implementing an SCF solution if its non-OECD purchase volume is estimated to be greater than $3,373,984.
- An exporting focal company generates potential savings by implementing an SCF solution if its non-OECD turnover volume is estimated to be greater than $1,904,937.

6.6 Interpretation of Results

Having calculated all benefits/revenue streams and the overall SCF market size the results of the applied SCF solution model are reflected and interpreted. Although the results shown in Tables 6.10 and 6.11 indicate the overall potential SCF

market size, the amount of net benefits to focal companies and their suppliers/
buyers must be interpreted differently. Up to this point, the potential savings to
supply chain constituents claimed a minimum volume of relevant transactions,
derived by the net benefit per A/P or A/R. This allows us to quantify a breakeven
level specified to a single company.

To derive more meaningful results from the total net benefit number, realistic
average amounts of payables/receivables to each focal company would have to be
assigned. Regarding suppliers and buyers the same should be done, but additionally the average number of suppliers/buyers per focal company should be
estimated, including possible overlaps. However, even more precise numbers
about the net benefits to each company would offer no direct inference towards the
deducible market potential for SCF solutions, because implications rely on further
company specifics. As indicated above, the direct additional contribution of total
net benefits is thereby assumed to be marginal.

Although the amount of tangible net benefits provides some explanation about
SCF market potential, there are numerous intangible benefits that facilitate more
sound conclusions. As indicated in Sect. 6.5, intangible benefits are mainly given
in the area of SCF key elements such as collaboration, transparency, demateral-
ization and automation. Altogether they are likely to further increase the application potential of SCF solutions. However, these intangible benefits are difficult
to quantify because they involve a vast number of factors and parameters.
Therefore, they have not been considered in this study.

Some assumptions have to be taken into account to interpret the obtained
results. Although the market size and market potential of SCF solutions has been
calculated based on market values, these should be rather regarded as rough
estimates because they rely on several assumptions. In the following, some of
these assumptions and necessary simplifications are discussed to enable a better
appraisal of the results of this study.

- The calculated market potential implies that each company either acts as an
  importer or exporter, thereby excluding the likely case that a company represents both. Therefore, the study does not consider presumable synergies
  regarding the implementation of SCF programs for import and export solutions.
  However, the likelihood of having an SCF program for a company in place for
  an import and export solution can be assumed to be rather small.
- A constraint can be seen in the generalization of the determined numbers, since
  original costs and potential cost savings are likely to vary significantly for each
  company, particularly in the different OECD countries. In addition, the calculations imply that transactions are made on credit terms excluding the possibility
  of prepayments.
- The geographic focus of this study is on OECD ⇔ non-OECD trading relationships, which can exclude existing market potential and thereby restrict
  market size. Since the SCF potential was analyzed and assumed to be more
  relevant for trade relationships between OECD and non-OECD companies, the
  calculated SCF market size does not consider intra-OECD and intra-non-OECD

trade respectively. Nevertheless, there is likely to be the potential for intra-OECD and domestic trade. This can be explained by the similar relevance of SCF goals and the positive, although presumably less significant, impact of SCF key elements such as better collaboration, transparency, dematerialization and automation. However, the funding benefits are likely to be smaller for OECD domestic trade because OECD companies can be assumed to have lower WACC and can obtain more competitive funding alternatives.

- Since it is a main goal of this study to describe and estimate the market size for SCF solutions, it does not take into consideration distinctions in the motif and benefit distribution of the different SCF solutions. Experience has shown, for instance, that the business logic for the application of an import or export solution model varies. Although an SCF solution model to an importer is often mainly taken up to support the suppliers in their funding, the benefits of extended DPO to the focal company might be negligible. By contrast, an SCF solution model to an exporter can generate a competitive advantage to the focal company because the offered solution is perceived by the buyer as fulfilling the supplier's selection criteria.

These assumptions and limitations demonstrate that the calculation of the total market size for SCF solutions and net benefits for supply chain constituents are characterized by a high level of complexity. Therefore, the applied assumptions provide the possibility of conducting a first step in looking for an approach to quantify the SCF market and its potential benefits for market participants.

References

Aberdeen Group (2007) The 2008 state of the market in supply chain finance. Aberdeen-Study, Boston

Atradius Corporate Communications (2007) Atradius Zahlungsbarometer—Studie zum Zahlungsverhalten europäischer Unternehmen. http://www.atradius.de/debitorenmanagement praxis/publikationen/zahlungsmoralbarometer.html. Accessed 09 Apr 2010

Barnes E, Dai J, Deng S, Down D (2000) Electronics manufacturing service industry. The Logistics Institute-Asia Pacific, Singapore

Bass HK, Ashish G, Iijima TJ (2002) What is the "true cost" of processing a freight bill? J Corp Account Finance 14(2):69–78

Celent Communications (2008) After the purchase order: easing pain points in B2B transactions. http://reports.celent.com/ResearchServices/reports.asp?ServiceID=3. Accessed 09 Apr 2010

Enslow B, Sadlovska V (2006) Supply chain finance benchmark report. Aberdeen-Study, Boston

Global Business Intelligence (2007) Global supply chain finance—first edition. www.eurofinance. com/pdf/GlobalSupply.pdf. Accessed 14 Aug 2008

Griesar J (2007) Study on the future opportunities and challenges of EU-China trade and investment relations—chemicals. http://www.development-solutions.eu/media/docs/reports/ Phase%202/Phase_2_4_Chemicals.pdf. Accessed 09 Apr 2010

Hirschman AO (1964) The paternity of an index. Am Econ Rev 54(5):761

Hofmann E (2010) Zum Wandel des Working Capital Managements in Supply Chains: ein Blick zurück und zukünftige Handlungsoptionen. In: Delfmann W, Wimmer T (Eds) Strukturwandel in der Logistik - Wissenschaft und Praxis im Dialog. Bobingen pp 249–273

IOMA (2003) IOMA quantifies A/p processing costs in 12 industries. Preview Financial Exec News 3(1):12

IOMA (2006) Exclusive IOMA survey: predicted merit pay increases hover at 3.6% in 2007. Preview Rep Salary Surv 6(8):1–13

Koch B (2009) E-invoicing & EBPP European market overview. http://www.billentis.com/ ebilling_e-invoicing_European_Market_Overview_2009.pdf. Accessed 09 Apr 2010

Lynch TM (1999) Globalization in the motor vehicle industry: final conference summary. MIT University Press, Cambridge

McClements J, Cranswick R (2001) World mining overview. www.resourcecapitalfunds.com/ rcf_wmo_031201.pdf. Accessed 09 Apr 2010

Miles JA, Ezzell JR (1980) The weighted average cost of capital, perfect capital markets, and project life: a clarification. J Financial Quant Anal 15(3):719–730

Myers R (2006) How low can it go? CFO Mag 22(10):79–88

New York Stern University (2008a) Total beta by industry sector. http://pages.stern.nyu. edu/~adamodar/New_Home_Page. Accessed 20 Oct 2008

New York Stern University (2008b) Costs of capital by industry sector. http://pages.stern.nyu. edu/~adamodar/New_Home_Page. Accessed 20 Oct 2008

New York Stern University (2010) Costs of capital by industry sector. http://pages.stern.nyu. edu/~adamodar/New_Home_Page. Accessed 09 Apr 2010

Nishimura K, Venditti A (2004) Capital depreciation, factor substitutability and indeterminacy. J Differ Equ Appl 10(13–15):1153–1169

Noble RD, Stern SA (1995) Membrane separations technology: principles and applications. Elsevier, Munich

OECD (2006) Balance of payments (MEI). http://stats.oecd.org/Index.aspx?DataSetCode= MEI_BOP. Accessed 09 Apr 2010

OECD (2008) Country risk classification. http://www.oecd.org/dataoecd/9/12/35483246.pdf. Accessed 09 Apr 2010

Reason T (2005) Capital ideas: the 2005 working capital survey. CFO Mag 21(12):88–92

UPS Capital (2006) Global supply chain finance. www.worldtrademag.com/WT/Home/Files/ PDFs/UPSCapital_World_Trade_byliner.pdf. Accessed 12 Aug 2008

Chapter 7
Concluding Remarks

Abstract The study's examination has revealed the significant relevance of SCF solutions. Especially, there is a growing interest among companies in optimizing their working capital structure whilst keeping up the continuity of the supply chain.

Keywords Future Research · Supply chain finance solutions · Market size · Working capital · Liquidity · Partner networks

7.1 Discussion

The main focus of this study was to quantify the relevance of SCF in terms of market size and benefits to supply chain constituents. Taking as a calculation basis the total worldwide transaction volume, several company and commercial relationship characteristics have been considered to further define the overall market size and benefits of SCF solutions.

The calculated benefits for a focal company and its suppliers (importer model) or buyers (exporter model) engaging in SCF show great potential for such solutions. Although the calculated cost savings and benefits for supply chain constituents are considerable, the market is still in its infancy. In a recent forum, the question came up of whether "supply chain finance was the elephant in the room" because although corporates recognize the potential value of such solutions, most have not seriously considered implementing one (Bramlet 2009). The main reasons for the slow uptake of SCF programs are that corporates still do not see the growing need for such solutions and financial institutions do not have the required expertise. This might now change.

The recent economic downturn has had a major impact on global supply chains. There is an increasing focus on working capital requirements as supply chain constituents take strong actions to manage their cash flows. In a recent survey, over 70% of respondents said their companies view working capital optimization as a high priority (Aberdeen Group 2008). Companies are increasingly looking carefully at how they manage their working capital by reducing their DSO and extending their payment terms towards their suppliers to help improve their cash flow. However, there is a growing recognition that this approach, focused only on the individual company, is resulting in a domino effect as suppliers and buyers respond by adopting similar measures with their supply chain partners (Deloitte 2008).

As a result, there is growing interest and the need for an approach that helps resolve this dilemma, helping companies manage their working capital while minimizing the risks of discontinuity in the supply chain. Nevertheless, over the past decade efforts have been made to improve the efficiency and effectiveness of supply chains, extending them into more distant and low cost geographies, using sophisticated analysis and planning routines to predict and meet future demand and refining international logistics. However, these improvements have mainly focused on the physical supply chain. In fact, it is often said that the physical supply chain has become just about as efficient as it can.

As a result of the current situation, where pressure on supply chains is growing because of the economic downturn but where refinements to the physical supply chain no longer have a significant impact, interest has been mounting on SCF solutions to ease the burden. Financial institutions, in particular, who are keen to lend but are reluctant to deteriorate their risk profiles further, are exploring innovative SCF solutions that include extending credit secured against robust assets, such as invoice debt (Kerle 2009).

Looking forward, with the global economy growing at a sound level, the trend of the increased use of SCF solutions will continue (Mutter 2010). However, the objective of companies will move from keeping an adequate liquidity level and improving working capital to increasing profitability, sales and market share.

Another trend that will continue and further increase in the coming years is the extension of partner networks between banks and service providers. Perhaps more than at any time in the past, financial institutions and SCF service providers have the opportunity to add value to their relationships by helping reducing the tensions that exist in the buyer–supplier relationship as everyone struggles to retain cash.

Most banks currently do not have the resources or expertise required to on-board trading partners into SCF programs, to operate cross-border finance transactions, to provide full visibility into transactions to mitigate the impact of supply chain disruptions proactively or to make prompt changes to data or processes based on new requirements or the varying levels of technical sophistication of the focal company. Therefore, the market will see a strong need for specialized SCF service providers to work closely with banks and credit risk insurers to provide the necessary expertise for professional SCF programs.

Looking further into the future, the new generation of SCF solutions will be further customized to the individual needs of the involved supply chain parties. Currently, there are standardized solution sets, i.e. one program servicing different company and need profiles. This means that the portfolio of participants is automatically reduced by the nature of a delimited standardized solution. In the future, the offering to individual focal companies will be more customized according to their balance sheet objectives, based on the need analysis of their portfolio and risk policies, as well as internal processes. Hence, the offering will be much more flexible and tailored to suit the individual customer profile (Mutter 2010).

Further emerging trends in the market are data-triggered finance solutions. These triggers can include POs, which can provide pre-shipment or WIP finance. A few players are emerging in this area using buyer POs for working capital facilities for key suppliers. Other triggers will include proof of delivery received through forwarders. As more cargo is shipped with electronic messages and advanced shipment notices, there will be more opportunities to develop liquidity off these messages (Gustin 2005).

7.2 Outlook

The intention of this study was to contribute to the emerging SCF research in the market by developing an approach to calculate the market size for SCF solutions. Although the estimated SCF market size and benefits for suppliers and buyers is based on several assumptions, the derivation of the need and types of SCF solutions and particularly the taxonomy of narrowing down the relevant number of transactions should give useful inspiration for more detailed research. The accomplishment of this study is intended to be a first roadmap, which offers guidance to approach relevant questions in this field.

Further studies in this field should focus on eliminating some of the discussed limitations. For instance, an approach to estimate the intra-OECD market potential of SCF solutions or a separate, more detailed focus on the differences between the import and export model might be of interest. It might also be attempted to further specify the size and industry of a potentially benefiting company, thereby not solely focusing on the focal company but the characteristics of the supplier/buyer company should equally be studied.

References

Aberdeen Group (2008) Working capital optimization: finance and supply chain strategies for today's business environment. Aberdeen-Study, Boston

Bramlet T (2009) How to win friends and influence supply chain finance. http://blogs.gxs.eu/2009/05/20/how-to-win-friends-and-influence-supply-chain-finance/. Accessed 12 Apr 2010

Deloitte (2008) Supply chain finance releasing working capital within the supply chain. http://www.deloitte.com/assets/Dcom-Switzerland/Local%20Assets/Documents/EN/Consumer%20Business/Consumer%20packaged%20goods/UK_CB_SupplyChainFinance.pdf. Accessed 09 Apr 2010

Gustin D (2005) Emerging trends in supply chain finance. World Trade 18(8):52

Kerle P (2009) The growing need for supply chain finance. http://www.gtnews.com/article/7625.cfm. Accessed 09 Apr 2010

Mutter (2010) The next generation of supply chain finance, gtnews. http://www.gtnews.com/article/7906.cfm. Accessed 22 Feb 2011

Annex

A1 OECD ⇔ Non-OECD Exports Per Country in 2006

Country	Food (and live animals)	Beverages and tobacco	Crude materials (except fuels)	Mineral fuels, lubricants and related materials
Australia	$5,374,148,197	$216,666,308	$12,693,284,989	$8,718,065,747
Austria	$874,383,290	$408,051,581	$290,445,373	$380,601,901
Belgium	$2,519,731,056	$144,376,548	$1,314,122,516	$1,092,785,201
Canada	$4,240,182,095	$53,333,239	$5,212,296,662	$734,478,398
Czech Republic	$343,126,483	$58,751,311	$171,710,044	$80,547,382
Denmark	$1,864,878,636	$50,254,720	$957,568,153	$222,731,363
Finland	$518,522,607	$68,242,788	$1,139,703,020	$338,211,446
France	$4,866,913,181	$2,061,187,469	$1,314,696,017	$3,002,599,474
Germany	$4,306,832,000	$1,219,764,000	$3,105,787,000	$690,664,000
Greece	$710,970,699	$294,815,683	$697,630,973	$1,716,930,344
Hungary	$1,216,566,000	$52,567,000	$162,779,000	$808,594,000
Iceland	$221,022,491	$174,046	$3,699,401	$15,752,427
Ireland	$1,424,642,534	$58,137,606	$150,979,009	$21,960,351
Italy	$2,474,161,045	$460,427,707	$1,464,710,610	$6,350,317,952
Japan	$1,622,317,743	$332,152,406	$5,047,001,127	$2,608,007,684
Korea	$849,519,705	$388,950,602	$2,036,029,794	$12,254,221,990
Luxembourg	$1,359,935	$1,802,912	$18,941,750	$49,432
Mexico	$781,451,888	$127,226,084	$928,498,106	$3,112,918,666
Netherlands	$5,606,698,536	$456,916,919	$2,965,870,417	$3,349,917,886
New Zealand	$4,377,878,499	$28,682,504	$1,066,359,375	$12,384,066
Norway	$1,465,741,420	$2,199,115	$199,219,958	$1,484,863,956
Poland	$2,187,627,431	$234,147,032	$333,639,647	$458,914,026
Portugal	$316,468,629	$275,866,310	$207,260,226	$188,239,313
Slovak Republic	$180,927,638	$8,365,436	$107,766,759	$61,443,422
Spain	$2,171,008,315	$440,045,501	$960,549,326	$2,114,881,831
Sweden	$372,435,166	$68,704,148	$1,197,731,263	$300,448,411

(continued)

(continued)

Country	Food (and live animals)	Beverages and tobacco	Crude materials (except fuels)	Mineral fuels, lubricants and related materials
Switzerland	$377,677,558	$318,692,357	$88,354,357	$145,562,043
Turkey	$1,923,320,377	$121,747,682	$543,250,535	$124,644,614
United Kingdom	$2,421,475,037	$2,299,152,761	$3,056,044,866	$10,589,265,574
United States	$17,418,997,949	$1,137,508,406	$22,829,758,160	$13,279,885,909

Country	Animal and vegetable oils, fats and waxes	Chemicals and related products	Manufactured goods	Machinery and transport equipment
Australia	$176,763,537	$2,403,573,676	$7,207,042,691	$4,623,569,016
Austria	$8,050,423	$2,555,624,212	$4,872,755,460	$10,246,018,751
Belgium	$82,135,995	$9,296,573,066	$15,730,013,975	$9,330,520,101
Canada	$161,055,188	$2,919,996,279	$3,470,129,792	$7,273,141,109
Czech Republic	$3,814,842	$1,063,611,894	$2,528,408,112	$5,492,333,815
Denmark	$58,637,090	$988,219,512	$725,679,654	$4,497,112,320
Finland	$11,791,468	$1,735,554,745	$4,339,097,990	$14,641,037,096
France	$73,534,083	$14,414,297,125	$10,114,798,940	$51,879,243,509
Germany	$208,824,000	$24,691,402,000	$26,954,352,000	$123,745,664,000
Greece	$37,913,461	$955,993,628	$1,788,200,817	$1,136,986,256
Hungary	$47,582,000	$2,389,566,000	$1,769,938,000	$7,508,804,000
Iceland	$2,729,893	$17,191,590	$17,147,868	$70,407,517
Ireland	$1,429,462	$1,910,032,185	$111,803,538	$5,267,861,128
Italy	$190,132,436	$7,640,736,449	$21,715,668,114	$42,387,347,462
Japan	$26,740,265	$32,408,823,636	$46,157,898,516	$184,571,430,525
Korea	$21,195,249	$24,874,404,769	$29,461,202,993	$105,998,150,697
Luxembourg	–	$33,760,880	$528,394,670	$526,831,761
Mexico	$13,511,149	$3,109,037,907	$2,674,873,267	$7,363,886,978
Netherlands	$157,410,777	$8,103,929,902	$3,908,823,641	$20,674,179,528
New Zealand	$59,015,353	$206,822,257	$573,020,997	$701,146,583
Norway	$4,997,653	$296,751,592	$801,668,238	$3,197,945,526
Poland	$29,970,949	$2,911,325,482	$5,633,576,991	$6,306,285,399
Portugal	$129,663,106	$314,959,579	$984,339,035	$2,441,851,772
Slovak Republic	$260,816	$404,576,991	$1,171,625,357	$1,998,871,537
Spain	$268,555,362	$4,629,643,689	$6,695,099,260	$14,293,414,523
Sweden	$19,523,307	$1,486,092,750	$3,654,532,442	$14,198,199,471
Switzerland	$4,944,801	$8,171,909,735	$2,819,251,454	$8,238,351,613
Turkey	$194,084,190	$1,198,630,672	$6,535,522,405	$2,608,946,327
United Kingdom	$69,696,549	$11,523,177,415	$12,656,605,586	$40,623,045,903
United States	$764,768,723	$34,836,707,394	$26,665,228,807	$166,553,304,750

Country	Miscellaneous manufactured articles	Commodities and transactions not classified elsewhere
Australia	$892,272,348	$13,442,966,944
Austria	$2,176,194,342	$868,332,858
Belgium	$1,945,857,178	$1,472,404,214
Canada	$1,273,483,389	$525,506,416
Czech Republic	$887,537,097	$146,604,384
Denmark	$1,095,665,009	$434,995,718
Finland	$1,161,641,902	$259,865,281
France	$8,794,439,117	$2,010,966,377
Germany	$17,429,292,000	$10,785,636,000
Greece	$1,138,880,016	$42,497,378
Hungary	$853,926,000	$4,616,000
Iceland	$6,051,035	$795,938
Ireland	$576,421,487	$222,082,176
Italy	$17,316,832,240	$611,682,155
Japan	$25,878,203,405	$17,222,584,475
Korea	$12,257,600,205	$584,249,179
Luxembourg	$90,259,336	$3,059,667
Mexico	$752,667,950	$16,573,172
Netherlands	$4,782,294,645	$347,749,062
New Zealand	$140,174,063	$207,280,071
Norway	$378,712,289	$1,567,175
Poland	$2,352,053,726	$138,457,546
Portugal	$504,745,644	$1,762,490,226
Slovak Republic	$348,966,469	$30,320,931
Spain	$3,415,016,276	$763,819,245
Sweden	$1,533,092,882	$1,205,825,879
Switzerland	$7,988,822,332	$33,720,681
Turkey	$2,548,087,508	$16,130,566,756
United Kingdom	$10,185,302,532	$4,056,655,247
United States	$29,339,768,576	$11,590,749,930

A2 OECD ⇔ Non-OECD Imports Per Country in 2006

Country	Food (and live animals)	Beverages and tobacco	Crude materials (except fuels)	Mineral fuels, lubricants and related materials
Australia	$1,898,465,729	$110,552,977	$726,586,898	$14,977,044,275
Austria	$943,077,959	$42,531,950	$549,339,356	$3,979,458,999
Belgium	$4,447,915,348	$166,971,043	$2,970,405,637	$7,943,428,462
Canada	$3,893,844,749	$293,901,269	$2,842,424,559	$11,826,668,727
Czech Republic	$508,472,891	$64,852,124	$1,090,330,083	$5,954,138,807
Denmark	$1,391,249,092	$162,227,362	$412,359,812	$1,395,359,275
Finland	$548,573,955	$59,066,104	$2,798,350,792	$6,969,707,156
France	$7,201,823,298	$219,298,931	$3,983,997,747	$43,832,480,723
Germany	$10,785,923,000	$869,388,000	$10,282,408,000	$39,562,330,000
Greece	$978,051,116	$108,569,510	$848,053,003	$10,845,390,277
Hungary	$269,134,000	$14,919,000	$395,826,000	$3,796,085,000
Iceland	$56,915,789	$4,274,707	$117,416,529	$88,233,064
Ireland	$493,468,695	$78,256,977	$419,610,673	$194,481,410
Italy	$6,034,833,511	$55,668,748	$6,802,160,466	$45,669,320,088
Japan	$21,119,596,208	$365,461,767	$23,767,641,652	$141,528,071,296
Korea	$5,419,415,749	$120,022,344	$9,768,556,166	$79,480,738,258
Luxembourg	$14,164,956	$712,303	$95,193,436	$98,719
Mexico	$1,385,588,713	$100,509,500	$1,784,937,937	$2,555,371,765
Netherlands	$6,936,739,617	$455,970,629	$5,032,735,969	$28,248,633,084
New Zealand	$455,615,708	$22,864,173	$171,655,732	$2,763,628,640
Norway	$838,096,821	$32,993,924	$1,748,455,234	$336,943,301
Poland	$1,822,689,450	$184,757,675	$1,716,977,576	$10,412,820,085
Portugal	$1,062,694,685	$19,568,355	$580,480,173	$6,955,344,023
Slovak Republic	$209,965,352	$9,093,633	$638,636,046	$4,719,713,906
Spain	$7,750,883,045	$441,395,272	$5,753,117,492	$40,239,618,492
Sweden	$816,303,700	$107,342,414	$1,070,890,073	$4,726,048,228
Switzerland	$1,029,626,993	$106,459,499	$176,799,393	$2,849,772,327
Turkey	$607,094,641	$71,778,286	$3,477,451,055	$6,044,201,698
United Kingdom	$13,331,342,212	$1,220,772,432	$5,426,225,790	$21,844,439,483
United States	$28,127,670,920	$1,830,233,393	$11,945,708,287	$203,394,617,937

Country	Animal and vegetable oils, fats and waxes	Chemicals and related products	Manufactured goods	Machinery and transport equipment
Australia	$165,307,690	$2,708,451,706	$6,367,756,209	$18,008,490,283
Austria	$38,653,519	$583,190,825	$2,283,585,148	$5,217,777,068
Belgium	$167,642,865	$4,346,141,586	$18,456,444,711	$7,091,539,051
Canada	$88,536,301	$2,080,758,679	$9,588,212,909	$21,627,666,268
Czech Republic	$15,588,973	$764,918,244	$2,082,066,349	$6,756,676,074
Denmark	$177,001,256	$333,522,998	$1,904,568,752	$3,418,973,726
Finland	$8,802,536	$918,595,516	$2,071,095,743	$6,807,685,962
France	$500,022,051	$6,020,669,044	$10,938,686,826	$27,616,742,080
Germany	$993,546,000	$6,677,427,000	$25,354,637,000	$70,521,301,000
Greece	$113,843,986	$754,679,131	$3,191,409,152	$1,865,458,880
Hungary	$16,337,000	$672,833,000	$1,447,964,000	$8,481,162,000
Iceland	$1,816,491	$39,923,526	$146,659,799	$217,429,263
Ireland	$28,098,798	$592,470,420	$761,584,942	$8,093,000,691
Italy	$1,147,295,364	$4,943,934,428	$26,849,423,289	$13,975,875,192
Japan	$540,266,029	$11,600,488,235	$35,647,885,396	$81,556,669,906
Korea	$352,892,432	$7,368,075,382	$23,374,372,421	$38,270,520,880
Luxembourg	$1,614	$52,677,506	$199,430,331	$267,875,858
Mexico	$239,875,443	$2,693,217,153	$8,059,447,779	$34,714,142,478
Netherlands	$1,386,802,868	$4,658,502,290	$8,569,467,007	$39,330,627,056
New Zealand	$51,903,832	$702,554,103	$1,146,849,175	$2,444,455,441
Norway	$116,141,014	$362,197,431	$2,242,196,019	$3,224,340,108
Poland	$97,368,315	$1,911,087,680	$4,181,712,155	$8,404,317,518
Portugal	$37,886,203	$370,427,301	$1,263,184,042	$960,946,655
Slovak Republic	$8,754,728	$300,969,816	$901,424,723	$2,049,399,115
Spain	$687,119,834	$3,613,069,277	$10,437,139,462	$14,840,029,015
Sweden	$103,412,514	$533,421,938	$2,354,450,706	$4,613,540,534
Switzerland	$44,799,569	$1,164,238,742	$3,979,236,313	$2,498,063,178
Turkey	$698,431,623	$3,765,662,708	$10,211,958,439	$5,783,862,102
United Kingdom	$734,254,282	$13,145,835,735	$23,762,405,979	$48,267,717,960
United States	$1,208,732,573	$30,389,397,272	$109,733,436,125	$238,943,407,733

Country	Miscellaneous manufactured articles	Commodities and transactions not classified elsewhere
Australia	$9,435,035,263	$4,637,715,074
Austria	$4,249,296,630	$404,913,011
Belgium	$9,159,383,795	$882,955,506
Canada	$15,558,587,607	$2,633,119,631
Czech Republic	$2,413,325,406	$162,361,101
Denmark	$3,945,420,643	$184,901,835
Finland	$2,054,277,367	$146,350,422
France	$24,880,923,229	$19,757,882
Germany	$37,901,364,000	$13,500,944,000
Greece	$1,711,296,579	$8,220,060
Hungary	$925,671,000	$43,778,000
Iceland	$218,705,669	$303,574
Ireland	$1,868,095,982	$106,024,377
Italy	$20,224,809,658	$1,671,117,691
Japan	$50,218,426,205	$6,747,153,581
Korea	$10,270,858,011	$603,146,848
Luxembourg	$170,191,685	$3,664,135
Mexico	$6,890,424,702	$1,874,196,380
Netherlands	$9,909,942,679	$1,612,047
New Zealand	$1,708,587,462	$49,239,927
Norway	$2,899,691,098	$44,001,585
Poland	$2,974,347,271	$2,555,517,708
Portugal	$514,606,193	$2,432,286,974
Slovak Republic	$1,482,069,118	$1,905,253
Spain	$13,442,704,196	$196,187,475
Sweden	$3,852,515,066	$165,876,408
Switzerland	$4,339,542,285	$711,524,321
Turkey	$2,455,526,976	$31,937,199,985
United Kingdom	$37,216,656,628	$1,837,326,617
United States	$191,053,787,012	$17,283,557,672

A3 Invoice Processed and Value Per Industry 2006 (Aberdeen Group, 2006)

Industry	Average # of invoices processed monthly	Average value of invoices processed each month ($)
Manufacturing	2,385	5,636,000
High tech	2,853	4,190,650
Finance	4,478	2,076,475
Distribution	2,120	205,250
Telecommunication	555	1,732,000
Wholesale	2,221	635,400
Aerospace and defense	1,069	4,867,900
Automotive	3,150	1,331,150
Mining and energy	5,537	1,073,725
Pharmaceuticals	1,027	3,492,325
Media	2,665	133,500
Retail	2,629	109,500
Chemicals	8,919	165,625
Computer equipment	6,400	8,083,500
Consumer electronics	3,349	206,500
Packaging	3,056	10,586,500
Construction–engineering	2,993	4,383,400
Education	4,102	1,669,500
Food and beverage	3,009	214,275
Metals	2,793	4,785,450
Average	5,392	4,367,125

A4 Days Inventory Held (DIH) Per Industry

Industry	1996	1997	1998	1999	2000	2001	2002	2003	2004	2005	N
Oil and gas producers	26	23	25	23	17	19	21	21	19	21	158
Oil equipment, services and distribution	33	33	26	32	32	29	30	24	27	30	96
Chemicals	73	74	75	77	73	73	73	69	70	67	371
Forestry and paper	74	76	71	73	72	70	68	64	64	66	88
Industrial metals	90	86	87	87	89	89	87	79	84	85	219
Mining	70	63	62	72	60	72	68	73	70	67	62
Construction and materials	70	69	70	69	71	67	63	60	60	60	524
Aerospace and defense	105	103	108	104	106	107	100	93	99	102	88
General industrials	67	72	73	74	69	66	65	64	66	65	175
Electronic and electrical equipment	90	89	90	89	90	87	85	79	82	76	459
Industrial engineering	90	90	90	90	90	90	86	83	84	78	436
Industrial transportation	5	5	4	4	5	4	5	4	4	5	173
Support services	16	16	15	16	13	11	11	10	12	6	303
Automobiles and parts	56	55	58	55	56	55	51	52	53	50	221
Beverages	56	58	58	57	59	63	62	62	57	56	102
Food producers	51	55	52	52	54	54	54	53	52	56	378
Household goods	94	95	90	90	95	88	88	85	85	87	248
Leisure goods	95	92	91	85	81	78	78	77	73	72	113
Personal goods	100	102	101	101	100	98	92	96	94	95	353
Tobacco	142	132	124	130	127	125	132	122	136	134	24
Health care equipment and services	76	73	76	83	82	78	79	83	84	77	296
Pharmaceuticals and biotechnology	87	89	88	89	87	98	97	95	102	105	214
Food and drug retailers	33	33	35	35	33	32	32	31	31	31	101
General retailers	70	69	70	69	67	65	63	64	65	67	379
Media	25	22	20	21	21	20	17	18	17	16	202
Travel and leisure	12	12	10	11	11	11	11	11	10	10	328
Fixed line telecommunications	18	17	15	16	17	14	10	10	12	11	63
Mobile telecommunications	20	19	21	16	23	21	13	18	22	18	31
Electricity	28	27	24	26	20	16	21	18	19	18	133
Gas, water and multiutilities	27	26	24	25	25	22	23	21	23	24	95
Software and computer services	13	10	8	7	4	3	2	2	2	1	285
Technology hardware and equipment	89	89	84	87	91	80	76	73	78	73	478
Average	59	59	58	58	57	56	55	54	55	54	

A5 Days Sales Outstanding (DSO) Per Industry

Industry	1996	1997	1998	1999	2000	2001	2002	2003	2004	2005	N
Oil and gas producers	65	59	59	69	63	47	58	50	53	54	158
Oil equipment, services and distribution	79	77	72	83	82	74	75	74	78	84	96
Chemicals	85	87	77	81	81	79	76	73	72	72	371
Forestry and paper	68	73	76	82	75	73	65	65	64	63	88
Industrial metals	76	76	72	77	74	65	65	64	60	60	219
Mining	52	56	56	52	48	49	48	47	50	48	62
Construction and materials	91	94	92	92	91	88	87	82	82	83	524
Aerospace and defense	74	70	69	73	73	70	68	69	69	68	88
General industrials	72	73	67	70	70	70	68	68	68	68	175
Electronic and electrical equipment	80	81	80	83	84	75	79	78	77	77	459
Industrial engineering	91	91	91	94	94	91	88	88	87	86	436
Industrial transportation	55	57	57	58	59	54	53	50	52	52	173
Support services	71	69	69	69	70	64	61	63	64	62	303
Automobiles and parts	70	72	71	71	71	68	68	68	67	68	221
Beverages	52	55	54	56	55	55	53	53	54	57	102
Food producers	50	49	48	48	50	49	47	46	45	46	378
Household goods	63	65	61	66	66	63	61	63	62	61	248
Leisure goods	68	68	65	64	63	62	59	56	54	52	113
Personal goods	71	74	70	71	70	66	65	60	58	59	353
Tobacco	32	38	39	27	35	34	35	46	42	42	24
Health care equipment and services	75	73	75	75	71	70	63	64	63	62	296
Pharmaceuticals and biotechnology	77	79	77	83	81	78	69	76	73	75	214
Food and drug retailers	10	10	12	11	11	12	12	11	11	11	101
General retailers	19	20	19	18	17	17	16	15	16	15	379
Media	72	72	71	74	72	67	64	66	65	67	202
Travel and leisure	25	25	26	26	27	27	26	25	25	24	328
Fixed line telecommunications	79	78	72	77	79	75	66	59	55	57	63
Mobile telecommunications	67	67	57	64	66	61	58	48	43	46	31
Electricity	59	56	53	59	74	59	60	58	59	60	133
Gas, water and multiutilities	56	52	49	56	57	46	54	55	54	58	95
Software and computer services	89	89	89	87	90	78	76	76	78	76	285
Technology hardware and equipment	72	79	73	78	75	66	66	68	63	66	478
Average	65	65	63	65	65	61	60	59	58	59	

A6 Days Payables Outstanding (DPO) Per Industry

Industry	1996	1997	1998	1999	2000	2001	2002	2003	2004	2005	N
Oil and gas producers	75	68	56	77	67	57	67	57	69	66	158
Oil equipment, services and distribution	53	52	48	50	51	45	45	40	44	48	96
Chemicals	61	60	61	60	59	58	56	58	58	56	371
Forestry and paper	51	50	48	48	49	48	43	42	42	46	88
Industrial metals	46	50	45	48	48	46	46	45	46	43	219
Mining	48	46	43	40	43	48	47	46	50	46	62
Construction and materials	62	65	65	64	64	65	64	61	62	62	524
Aerospace and defense	44	42	42	43	43	43	39	40	40	41	88
General industrials	48	49	50	50	52	49	49	47	51	51	175
Electronic and electrical equipment	50	52	52	54	59	51	50	52	53	54	459
Industrial engineering	61	60	61	58	62	57	56	59	64	61	436
Industrial transportation	40	39	37	37	37	38	37	35	34	36	173
Support services	37	38	38	36	37	33	32	33	34	33	303
Automobiles and parts	56	59	58	58	63	58	58	57	57	60	221
Beverages	49	50	47	51	51	50	48	51	48	52	102
Food producers	38	40	37	40	40	41	40	39	39	40	378
Household goods	47	46	47	49	48	49	48	49	51	49	248
Leisure goods	47	49	44	49	50	45	47	47	47	46	113
Personal goods	54	55	49	53	51	47	50	47	48	48	353
Tobacco	40	39	38	42	36	38	36	36	38	33	24
Health care equipment and services	45	45	47	47	44	44	41	41	41	40	296
Pharmaceuticals and biotechnology	58	59	60	64	62	64	65	62	69	71	214
Food and drug retailers	36	34	36	35	36	36	33	34	35	36	101
General retailers	46	45	44	44	44	44	42	42	44	43	379
Media	58	54	58	63	58	57	53	50	51	51	202
Travel and leisure	35	34	33	33	34	30	32	31	31	31	328
Fixed line telecommunications	93	86	97	96	118	95	98	83	69	82	63
Mobile telecommunications	77	81	75	74	94	98	69	71	68	65	31
Electricity	46	45	50	49	54	48	57	48	48	50	133
Gas, water and multiutilities	51	46	45	45	53	37	47	47	45	51	95
Software and computer services	55	54	53	47	48	45	46	44	44	44	285
Technology hardware and equipment	58	59	54	64	62	50	53	57	58	57	478
Average	52	52	50	52	54	50	50	49	49	50	

A7 Cash Conversion Cycle (CCC) Per Industry

Industry	1996	1997	1998	1999	2000	2001	2002	2003	2004	2005	N
Oil and gas producers	16	14	29	16	13	10	12	14	4	10	158
Oil equipment, services and distribution	60	59	50	65	63	58	60	58	61	65	96
Chemicals	97	100	91	99	95	94	93	85	84	83	371
Forestry and paper	91	99	98	106	98	95	90	87	87	83	88
Industrial metals	120	112	114	116	115	107	106	99	98	102	219
Mining	74	73	75	85	66	73	69	73	71	69	62
Construction and materials	99	98	97	97	98	90	86	81	80	81	524
Aerospace and defense	135	132	136	134	136	135	128	122	129	128	88
General industrials	90	95	91	95	87	87	84	84	83	82	175
Electronic and electrical equipment	120	118	119	118	114	112	113	105	105	99	459
Industrial engineering	119	121	121	126	122	124	118	112	108	103	436
Industrial transportation	20	23	24	24	26	20	21	19	22	20	173
Support services	50	47	47	49	46	42	40	40	42	34	303
Automobiles and parts	70	68	72	68	64	66	60	63	63	58	221
Beverages	59	63	65	62	63	68	68	65	62	61	102
Food producers	63	64	63	61	63	63	61	61	58	62	378
Household goods	110	114	105	107	113	102	101	99	96	99	248
Leisure goods	115	111	113	101	93	95	90	86	80	78	113
Personal goods	117	121	122	119	119	117	107	109	104	106	353
Tobacco	135	132	125	115	126	122	130	132	139	144	24
Health care equipment and services	106	102	104	111	108	104	102	106	105	99	296
Pharmaceuticals and biotechnology	106	109	105	108	107	112	102	109	106	109	214
Food and drug retailers	7	9	11	11	8	8	10	9	7	6	101
General retailers	43	45	44	42	40	38	37	37	37	39	379
Media	40	40	32	32	35	30	27	34	31	32	202
Travel and leisure	2	3	4	4	4	8	5	5	5	4	328
Fixed line telecommunications	4	8	−9	−3	−21	−6	−21	−14	−2	−15	63
Mobile telecommunications	9	5	3	7	−4	−15	2	−5	−3	−2	31
Electricity	41	38	27	36	40	27	24	28	30	28	133
Gas, water and multiutilities	33	31	29	35	29	31	31	28	32	31	95
Software and computer services	47	45	44	47	46	35	32	34	36	33	285
Technology hardware and equipment	104	109	103	101	105	97	90	84	83	82	478
Average	72	72	70	72	69	67	65	64	64	63